Child of the Cult
By Nori Muster

Copyright 2012; revised 2015. Nori Muster, the author, retains all rights to the content and design of this book.
Kindle Paperback edition 2017.
ISBN 9781520660431

Definition of the Term "Dangerous Cult"

Throughout this book, I use the terms "cult" and "dangerous cult" to describe authoritarian networks constructed around dangerous people who portray themselves as spiritual leaders. Authoritarianism in this context refers to the worst groups, where the leaders exhibit extraordinary dominance, abuse, and exploitation over their followers.

Table of Contents

A Childhood of Slavery in the Children of God
Jane Doe

Conclusion:
Deescalating the Cult Dynamic in Society

Appendices

Author's Acknowledgements

I want to thank Gina, Flore, Ananda, Ann, and Jane, the writers who told their stories for this collection. It takes inner strength to share difficult childhood experiences, and I believe their courage will inspire others. The contributors took part in writing their chapters, and Gina read the final manuscript, acting as the midwife, bringing the book into the world, and giving it the blessings of the children.

My study of children raised in cults began in 1994, when I learned the true history of the group I was in, ISKCON, the International Society for Krishna Consciousness. Through the nineties, I listened to the children's stories and collected their writings. The key writers I followed were Dylan Hickey (Nirmal-chandra), John Giuffre (Raghunatha Anudas), Srimad B. McKee, and the late Ananda McClure (taped interview). I appreciate and love all the children of ISKCON who accepted me as one of their own in the 1990s. I also want to thank Windle Turley, JD, and his legal team, who pursued justice for the children of ISKCON.

I would also like to thank the people who wrote their stories for my research, but did not grow up in a dangerous cult, or did not want their stories published. Their writing contributed to my research: Lisa W., M.Ed., LPC, CRC, Julie Star, MBA, and Julia L.F., Ph.D. All the subjects I worked with in the course of this study were in recovery, or entered recovery during the time I knew them. Furthermore, several had parents or gurus die during the time we worked together. They shared their innermost thoughts with me during these landmark events in their lives.

I first learned about child abuse and recovery in graduate school at Western Oregon University (1990-1992). I would like to thank my thesis committee, Victor Savicki, Ph.D., Merle Kelley, Ph.D., and Stephen Gibbons, Ph.D. for their guidance and support. During those years I also attended art therapy workshops at Marylhurst University and volunteered as an art teacher at Hillcrest Juvenile Reform School, and other agencies. I want to thank Professors David Calof, DAPA, and Janie Rhyne, ATR-BC, HLM, two of my teachers from Marylhurst who made a lasting impression on my studies. The late Virginia Axline, pioneer of play therapy, was one of my most important teachers in graduate school, even though I only met her through her writings.[1]

The International Cultic Studies Association (ICSA), the leading academic group that tracks cults, was instrumental in helping me research and write this book. I would like to thank Executive

Director Michael Langone, Ph.D., Lorna Goldberg, MSW, LCSW, Lois Kendall, Ph.D., Livia Barden, MSW, Steven Alan Hassan, M.Ed., LMHC, Brian Birmingham (researcher), Janja Lalich, Ph.D., and Carol Giambalvo. Attorneys from ICSA who provided feedback were Phil Elberg, J.D., Al Scheflin, J.D., and Robin Boyle Laisure, J.D. I also want to thank David and Mary Lee Cole of Bay Tree Publishing, whom I met through ICSA, for helping me complete the manuscript. I want to thank my fellow writer and ex-ISKCON friend, Steven Gelberg, MDiv., who is also affiliated with ICSA. Steve has read this and other manuscripts for me over many years.

Special thanks to Elizabeth Dulany, the acquisitions editor from the University of Illinois Press. She found my inquiry letter for *Betrayal of the Spirit* in 1994 and worked with me to see the book through to publication. Then she asked me to write a book about the children. Now I have written it, after fifteen years of research and many drafts.

I also want to thank Kendra Boileau. When she was an acquisitions editor for the University of Illinois Press, she got academic feedback for the manuscript. The insights in the critique proved instrumental to completing the book. My main academic advisor, Pam Broido, M.Ed., of the University of New Hampshire, devoted many hours to working with me and with the writers.

Deepest gratitude to Lois Kendall (from ICSA) and my mother, Paula Hassler, and for helping me decide how to present the children's stories. Many thanks to Srimad B. McKee, who read the manuscript early on and suggested the title, *Child of the Cult*. I also want to thank Pam Rector for line editing the final version.

Throughout the years of writing, I drew inner guidance from Elisabeth Kubler-Ross, M.D. (1926-2004), the pioneer in the field of death and dying. Like her, I chose my subject of study because few people wanted to talk about it. It took courage for her to speak out on death, a taboo subject at the time, and I have tried to follow in her footsteps speaking out about another difficult subject: child abuse.

My other guiding light for this book was Adolf Ogi, former president of Switzerland. In 2004, I saw him explain his vision[2] that if we could raise one generation of children with the principles of cooperation, then they would create world peace when they grow up. It sounds utopian, but we owe it to future generations to make this world safer for children. Meanwhile, we can at least learn to detect child abuse sooner and do more to help the victims.

On the Outside Looking In:
An Unblessed Child in the Unification Church
Flore A., Ph.D.

When Flore A. was two years old her parents joined the Unification Church and she grew up within the group into her teen years. She is now an anthropologist in Norway, writing about addiction, and studying addicts as stigmatized outsiders. Her upbringing gives her keen insights into her subjects. As a child she was a stigmatized outsider under a strict racial caste system. She remembers her life as "one long, never-ending major crisis" because she lived in four countries under a series of about twenty caretakers.[3]

I met Flore in 2005 after I found her autobiographical essay in the *Cultic Studies Review*, one of the ICSA publications.[4] We corresponded and she agreed to update her story and participate in my research.

Group Profile

The Rev. Sun Myung Moon (1920-2012) first established his organization in Seoul, South Korea, in 1954, as The Holy Spirit Association for the Unification of World Christianity (HSA-UWC). Now the group prefers the name Unification Church (UC) and stated in 2009 that they do not like to be called Moonies, a nickname the group acquired in the 1970s. Members refer to the group as "the family."

Rev. Moon is his followers' messiah and the philosophy is detailed in his book, *The Divine Principle*, which he wrote between 1935 and 1946. The doctrine combines Christian and Asian philosophies of the creation, fall, and redemption of humankind. Moon presents himself as a Christ figure and his followers fight against the world's evil forces, personified as Satan. The group claims as many as three million members, mostly in Korea and Japan.

Due to the original sin of Adam and Eve, called the fall, Moon contends that all unblessed people are sinful. To atone for sin, unblessed followers must pay indemnity through personal suffering. This involves showing endurance in the face of personal misfortune, as well as penance such as fasting, cold showers, rising early, fervent prayer, studying Moon's teachings, fundraising, and recruiting for the group. The atonement is severe; fasting may mean no food of any kind for three weeks.

The only way to completely remove the stain of original sin, according to Moon, is the blessing, where he arranges marriages between disciples in a ceremony called the matching, and then he marries the blessed couples in mass ceremonies in stadiums and other venues.[5] Anyone born from a union outside of a blessed marriage is considered sinful since the group considers sex outside of blessed marriages worse than murder.

Flore's Childhood Memories

Flore grew up as an unblessed child because she was born before her parents joined.[6] However, she said, "I decided at a relatively early age that I was surrounded by a group of gibbering morons." Even though she thinks this was "not the most sophisticated strategy," it was the most rational way to think about it and her attitude protected her. She could block out Rev. Moon's threats of hell and eternal damnation, which she thought of as ranting and raving in the "conceptual reality tunnel" of the group. In regards to the fall of Adam and Eve and the resulting consequences, she said:

> All this because of one badly timed and somewhat bungled-up sex act. I remember thinking that God must be incredibly cruel to punish us so severely for a

mistake that anyone can make. After all, they were only teenagers (according to *The Divine Principle*).

Although rational, Flore was lonely. She recalled:

> My mother was away for years, and even though she did call and visit sometimes, it took me a while to realize that she was my mother. I used to call her the same name as all the other kids did.

Flore's father was not a constant in her early life, either. She first met him when she was five, then he came and went, finally leaving the organization for good when she was twelve.

Flore's mother characterized her neglect of her daughter as a sacrifice for the greater good. She felt confident she was assigning Flore into God's hands and paid holy installments of prayer toward Flore's sacred life insurance (to use the group's language). The parents loved their children, but blindly trusted a system that betrayed them.

A child in a system like the UC feels emotional stress trying to fit in. Flore said it in these words:

> Throughout my childhood, youth, and especially during that last encounter with the church [mid-teens], I felt like I was gradually pressed further and further into a cramped box. A rather uncomfortable feeling when every part of my being just wanted to fly and soar freely across an infinite sky.

Flore's darkest hour as a child was when she had to leave a childhood friend who acted as her protector. She recalled,

He was the only person I ever became really attached to, and the day I heard that I was moving away from him was one of the worst days of my life. After all, I had no one else to love, and when we were separated it was as if part of my heart had been ripped out. I don't think I ever fully recovered from that shock. I still cry to this day when I think about it. I never forgot him, and every little death since then became almost painless in comparison, because until I gave birth to my son, I never [felt love . . .] again.

To make matters worse, they sent her off with a man from the group who did not speak German (her language at the time) and appeared to not like children. She said,

I remember standing alone in the dark somewhere in London surrounded by suitcases while he went off to buy tickets or something, and being completely overwhelmed by a wave of loss and pain. I started to cry uncontrollably when something very bizarre took place that I still remember with a smile. A group of black men all wearing shiny white suits saw me and came over to try and console me. Unfortunately, I didn't understand a word of what they were saying either, so they started to sing. I guess they must have been musicians. They just stood there in their glittering white suits and sang and sang and sang for what seemed like an eternity, just for me. I'll never forget that experience. Although they couldn't stop the tears from flowing or take away my pain, they certainly did catch my attention.

Flore said when she was thirteen she was expelled from Camp Sunrise, a Unification Church summer camp, for what she describes as defiant and unruly attitudes. At the beginning of a ceremony the adults said anybody who could not take the ritual seriously should leave. So she got up and left. Soon after, they dragged her back in by

14

her ear (physical abuse) and shamed her. They told her she was a bad influence on the blessed children, and accused her of trying to seduce the boys by not wearing a bra (sexual humiliation).

Flore's first attempt to leave the Church was at age fourteen, when she moved in with her ex-member father in California. She attended public high school, but felt lonely and empty. She said she could identify with another ex-cult child she read about who said it was like growing up confined to a space ship, then one day leaping out into space.

Finally, after an unusually lucid dream about Paris, she asked her father to buy her a one-way ticket to France. There she joined her mother selling orchids and recruiting new members on the streets. During her stay in France she attempted to be a good devotee, however, she said:

> After many months of endless debates, fights, and far too many unanswered questions, I finally realized that it just wasn't going to happen. *The Divine Principle* just wasn't equipped to encompass the whole kaleidoscope of realities that made up my weird and wonderful world.

On several occasions as a child, she tried to accept the philosophy. However, she said,

> I just couldn't muster up the necessary faith and devotion to become a long-term believer. I couldn't bring myself to see anything more extraordinary [in Rev. Moon] than an energetic Korean guy with strong charisma and impressive leadership abilities (and of course reproductive abilities), whom I held largely responsible for the sad and unpleasant state of affairs that my life had become.

Flore, now a doctor of anthropology, said she still must grapple with her childhood issues, but she does so with a positive attitude.

She said,

> I refuse to see myself as a passive victim. I believe that
> within every human being lies a field of unlimited
> potential, but tapping into that field sometimes means
> weathering extreme circumstances. Although many of
> my experiences as a child were due to circumstances
> beyond my control, I did have a choice in terms of how
> I chose to react to those circumstances, and that makes
> all the difference.

Caste System of the Unification Church Children

The true children, the highest rung in the caste system, were Rev. Moon's fourteen biological children and the children born of his blessed couples. Moon wanted to wipe out distinct non-Korean races, so he arranged mostly mixed-race marriages to produce interracial children. However, he would marry only Koreans to Koreans. The only exception was non-Korean blessed children could marry Korean blessed children.

All members refer to each other as true brothers and sisters with Rev. Moon and his wife as the true mother and father. Members think of the group as their real family and cut ties with their families of origin when they join.

In the UC's rigid hierarchical world, children learned from an early age whether they were blessed or unblessed. Due to the strict nature of the system, a child's station in life defined his or her existence within the group. There was no way for children to hide their unblessed-ness because it was a closed system where everyone knew each other.

Unification Church members shared strong attitudes about what it meant to be unblessed and it was a form of discrimination that would diminish a child's chances for a successful life within the group. On the inside there would be privileges and responsibilities the unblessed would never enjoy. The blessed children recited the pledge of the families in the morning services, had special seats of honor at the celebrations, and spent several years living in Korea, beginning at age ten to twelve. Blessed children were exempt from fundraising and recruitment duties, but tended to grow up dependent upon the group into adulthood. Many typically remain in the group to raise their own children. The blessed children carry the burden of what Flore calls "holy super kids." Moon taught them the whole world hangs on their prayers. Suffering and discord exist in the world only because the blessed children do not take their role seriously enough.

Flore's Healing

Flore felt lucky she was an outsider to the inner circle. When she left the UC once and for all, she moved ahead without fear of the group or whether non-cult people would judge her. She emerged as an individual following a path she chose for herself. In Norway she has found a place to call home, which proves ex-cult children may lead as normal a life as anyone else from any background.

The individual with the cult upbringing must define for him or herself what the experience will mean and what life will become when they leave. Well-intentioned family and helping professionals may do further damage if they tell a young person what they should be once they leave the group.

Bear in mind, by the time a person has left a dangerous group the acute psychological work might already be done, especially if the ex-member can get out of denial and see the group's problems realistically. Flore survived her childhood thanks to her rational thoughts during the experience.

Instead of believing the Unification Church dogma, Flore followed something inside she calls her inner voice. It did not speak to her in words, but she described it as a sense of original goodness and purity she found within herself that outweighed the stigma of original sin and unblessedness placed upon her in the group. She realized a real spiritual teacher would facilitate a bond between an individual and the person's own inner guidance, rather than a dependence upon a charismatic leader. Although her intuition told her there was something wrong with Rev. Moon, as a child she had no way to realize the extent of the predicament she was in, growing up in a dangerous religious cult with apocalypse-driven aspirations.

17

Dark Side of Rev. Moon

Besides Moon's role as the leader of his flock, he was alleged to have had underworld ties in Japan, and to have worked for the CIA. During the Vietnam years he organized pro-war groups on college campuses. He resented American-style representative government, and believed his destiny was to unify North and South Korea as a theocracy, hence the name Unification Church. After that was accomplished, he would unify the entire world under himself as the messiah. To that end, he started the *Washington Times* newspaper in Washington, DC, in 1982. Moon claimed he directed American politics through his media influence.[7] In 20000, his media company, News World Communications, purchased United Press International (UPI), a major newswire service.

Moon spent the last three years of his life fighting over the role of the *Washington Times*, and whether to continue subsidizing the newspaper. From 1982 to 2009, Moon had invested an estimated $2 billion to keep the newspaper going. In 2009, the organization announced Moon was turning operations over to his heirs. Justin Moon, the son chosen to run the family's operations in Asia, cut off the $35 million annual subsidy to the *Washington Times*. Justin Moon fired all the executives and the paper went into turmoil. Then in late 2010, the elderly Moon bought the paper back for $1.[8] Moon died in 2012. Although children in the organization were probably unaware of organizational machinations, children are the weakest link and may suffer the most stress. I feel compassion for those children born into the Unification Church post-9/11, because they were coming of age against a backdrop of organizational strife.

The aspiration for world domination is perhaps the most troubling aspect of the Unification Church. Researchers and ex-members report that the UC does not inflict extreme systemic physical and sexual abuse on children. Still, they condone some physical and sexual abuse, and they impose their fundamentalist views and caste system on their children. Listening to people who grew up in the microcosm of the Unification Church gives us fair warning of what it would be like to live in a world controlled by totalitarian leaders like Rev. Moon.

Coming of Age in the Age of Enlightenment: A Voice for the Voiceless in Transcendental Meditation
Gina C., M.S., N.P., CNM

Gina C. grew up in the Transcendental Meditation organization, commonly known as TM. She and her younger brother received TM initiation when they were eight and five, respectively. The mantra is supposed to be personal and kept secret, but on Gina's initiation day one of the other children blurted out his mantra shortly after receiving it. It was a moment of disillusionment for Gina because she realized the initiator had given all the children the same mantra. Nevertheless, she persisted on the organization's periphery until age thirty.

Today, Gina is a nurse practitioner and nurse-midwife, raising her children in the San Francisco Bay Area. I met Gina through the

ICSA when she contacted me to participate in my research.

Group Profile

Maharishi Mahesh Yogi (1917-2008),[9] born Mahesh Prasad Varma, started teaching Transcendental Meditation in 1958. It evolved into Maharishi Vedic Education Development Corporation (MVED), now a global network of meditation centers, businesses, schools, and health spas, said to be worth several billion dollars.[10] The Maharishi was the quintessential guru with long hair and beard, flowers, and flowing robes. He had it all: the secret to enlightenment, charisma, famous followers, and a scientific method to reach nirvana.

Although he portrayed himself as a celibate mystic, the Maharishi was notorious for putting sexual pressure on female followers. In 1968, actress Mia Farrow and musicians Donovan, Mike Love, Ravi Shankar, and the Beatles traveled to Maharishi's International Academy of Meditation at Rishikesh, India. According to sixties legend, the Maharishi made sexual advances on Mia Farrow. Learning of this, the Beatles went to the Maharishi and announced they were leaving. The Maharishi asked why, and John Lennon said, "If you're so cosmic, you'll know why."[11] As he was packing, Lennon wrote the song *Sexy Sadie*. At first he called it *Maharishi*, so the original lyrics would have read: "Maharishi what have you done, you made a fool of everyone." According to legend, bandmate

George Harrison persuaded Lennon to change the title, since George still considered Maharishi a genuine guru. That is how Maharishi got the nickname Sexy Sadie.

Like many dangerous cults, TM spread anti-child, anti-woman rhetoric. It started in the early days of the movement, when Maharishi explained children would distract devotees' attention from the more important pursuit of enlightenment. Thus, whole branches of the TM organization developed around celibacy where families were excluded.

Gina's Family History in the Group

Gina's parents joined TM early on, before there were any centers or schools, and became very active in 1965. They turned their home into an ashram, or home-based TM center, and held TM functions, such as initiation ceremonies, group meditations, lectures, and seasonal gatherings. Gina and her brother attended public school and participated in TM activities at home, where people regarded them as children of the age of enlightenment. People in the group believed that to be initiated at a young age meant a person had to have a certain kind of good karma. Plus the initiation had taken place at the Beverly Hills home of Roland and Helena Olson, celebrities within the group. Gina said,

> It was heady to be spiritual royalty. When my brother
> and I parroted Maharishi's teachings, an easy task from

lifelong immersion, surrounding adults were incredulous of lofty truths coming from the mouths of children!

But she recalled,

> My brother and I quickly tired of playing enlightened beings. We began visiting neighbors' homes during meditation functions. As an adolescent I often roamed the streets to avoid home initiation activities. I dallied with drifter teens on the streets, but avoided substance abuse. My teenage brother preferred to sleep in the back booths of fast-food restaurants where he worked, rather than return home at night to familial dysfunction.

Gina's mother traveled to Europe to attend advanced training courses for TM Initiators, repeatedly leaving her family behind for anywhere from six weeks to six months. In her mother's absence, Gina recalled,

> My working father, brother, and I cared for the home, groceries, and ourselves. The home was more stable without the active TM force determining domestic affairs.

But when her mother returned, Gina remembers,

> My mother heavily criticized our lack of domestic organization. We could never be good enough; she held us to TM's enlightened living standards in her absence. Nothing in daily family life could match the idealized life she had with Maharishi.

Gina had to suppress her discomfort with TM around her mother, but broke down in what she calls "violent emotional outbursts." This led to her living with various relatives and attending six different high schools with no mentor to guide her. As she recalled, she usually had to walk to various local high schools alone and register herself without a guardian's presence.

In 1974 at the age of fifteen, Gina moved in with her mother at the temporary campus of Maharishi International University (MIU) in Santa Barbara, California. Although she attended a public high school, her life revolved around happenings at the apartment complex that was the TM university campus. She recalled,

> The university consisted of college students, a few years older than me, studying a TM-based curriculum. I instantly had several hundred best friends! My mother remained preoccupied with her activities. I settled within the meditator social world, caring for the next crop of young TM children. I was MIU's valued teen princess, as TM's young adults envied me for my "youthful purity and elevated spiritual consciousness." Some also envied my parents' support of my cult involvement, while their parents criticized their involvement with Maharishi University.

People within the closed circle encouraged Gina to attend TM advanced training, but she refused. She said,

> Those who returned from prolonged programs no longer laughed. It seemed that their soft-spoken and somber attitude resulted from attempts to carry their meditative experience with them constantly. I wanted to enjoy life!

As Gina's mother prepared to attend one of the regular European advanced trainings, it was decided the best place for sixteen-year-old Gina to live was with the adult TM university meditating community. Gina's first teenage boyfriend was a much older MIU student, a Vietnam veteran. Decades later Gina realized this relationship met the legal definition of statutory rape. But as a teen, Gina found the relationship flattering and thought it was normal. Everyone in the Maharishi community accepted their involvement as a couple despite Gina's youth and their age difference.

At the age of eighteen, Gina married the man. She willingly participated since she believed the group's teachings that when two people had sex it was a sign they had exchanged past life karma with one another and marriage after a sexual encounter was appropriate. During the ceremony, she thought it would end in divorce, but said "I do" because she believed in the teachings. At age nineteen she had a child with him and massively hemorrhaged with an unlicensed midwife attending her home birth. TM members were against medical care; they thought meditating and eating the strict TM diet would give them what they called the Maharishi's perfect health. Gina ended the marriage a year later, after the man hit her.

In 1974, the Maharishi purchased an abandoned college campus in Fairfield, Iowa, and the residents of the Santa Barbara campus moved en masse to the new property. Non-cult residents of Fairfield were initially happy to learn someone had purchased the property. However, they were horrified several years later when Maharishi University allowed historic buildings to decay and eventually demolished them to make way for what they called enlightened architecture.

Apparently oblivious, TM leaders continued to tell their newest members the local people had always embraced them warmly. In fact, many Fairfield residents moved away to separate from the Maharishi influence. Others remained and benefited from the economic stimulus the Maharishi community provided.

In the 1970s, TM experienced unprecedented success in converting Westerners to meditation. As many as a thousand new initiates signed up in a single day at one of the group's many international locations. However, in the 1980s, TM's popularity spiraled dramatically downward, forcing once-vibrant centers to close and TM initiators to seek other employment. Those who stayed grew more isolated as the group became more eccentric. Gina explained,

Non-meditators' lives appeared irrelevant. Life on the outside could not compare with our noble purpose. Maharishi taught that non-meditators' lived in ignorance and involvement with non-meditators was akin to living in mud.

The group's lifestyle in Fairfield included hours of meditation, practicing what they called TM-Siddhis, defined as super-normal abilities of friendliness, infinite strength, celestial senses, and levitation. TM was already suffering from the cult stigma; taking up levitation did nothing to enhance their credibility. In addition, many members' children suffered increasing neglect. The Fairfield center had daycare facilities and childcare cooperatives, but some parents left their children unattended during meditation times.

Gina said, "After my own lonely childhood, I was disturbed by the hordes of neglected children." She tried to warn TM administrators, but said,

> I was deemed a troublemaker and was threatened with eviction from the movement, a frightening prospect at the time. So I stayed quiet.

Gina had a new husband and two more children by this time and skipped group meditations more often than she attended to provide her children with the attention she had missed in her own childhood. She recalled,

> My husband blamed his business failures on me because I did not meditate with the group. He said I generated bad karma for his businesses. When I was thirty, after yet another failed business attempt, I finally convinced him to leave the community to make a life elsewhere with our children and me.

After moving back to California and settling anew in the Bay

Area, Gina earned her bachelors in art history and a B.S. and M.S. in nursing and her nurse practitioner and nurse-midwife credentials, while working and raising her children. She and her husband eventually divorced. Gina went into medicine, providing women's health care. Her husband went out to look for another guru.

Although Gina was one of the first children to grow up in the Maharishi's aura, she has now left it behind. Rather than a childhood of happy memories, she vividly remembers the accepted trauma all around her: suicides, mental breakdowns, financial abuses, and predatory child abuse. Gina still loves her parents and acknowledges her friendships within the group. She also respects the religious idealism of her parents and others, and acknowledges, "many of TM group participants are kind, well intentioned people." However, she sees the cult dynamics that enable negligence, abuse, and violence. She said, "The group dynamic is seductive."

Vocal ex-TM members criticize the TM techniques, which were a combination of Hinduism and new age positive thinking. They say Maharishi used pseudo-scientific research to support his claims about the power of TM. Critics say the Maharishi was materialistic, attached to the money he made from selling ancient teachings. His legacy included allegations of tax fraud and offshore accounts. One former teacher, Joe Kellett, describes a deliberate pattern of fraud in the group, and that the group's practices could distort reality.[12]

Like the Rev. Moon and his blessed children, Maharishi taught his followers to blame themselves for everything going on in the world, from personal medical problems to international disasters. TM managers told members they had to be on time for meditation programs or risk causing earthquakes, riots, or wars. Group slogans such as, "What more can you do [to prevent the world's disasters]" and "Something terrible will happen [if you miss a vital meditation session]," reinforced the group's psychotic practice of self-blame.

The TM organization rejects clinical psychology, stating that all problems result from lifetimes of accumulated stress. They teach that the fastest and most effective way to remove these stresses is through their own trademarked brand of meditation. Any problems are discredited as mere side effects of rapid stress release or "unstressing." They claim continued TM meditation will cure all emotional problems.

A Voice for the Voiceless

An unanticipated result of Gina's recovery has been to speak publicly about how a cult upbringing affects children. She was surprised when ICSA Executive Director Michael Langone invited her to speak at a conference. She had not realized she could contribute something of value to the world's cult experts. Since that time she has presented at several ICSA conferences and other forums. The best way for silenced victims to come out of the shadows is to shine a light into those dark corners. Many of the children of TM are afraid to come forward, lest they be rejected or cause pain or embarrassment to their TM devotee loved ones. Gina still feels that concern, but chooses to speak for the damaged others, telling her story to give voice to the voiceless.

In 2007 Gina published an essay to explain how TM fits the criteria for thought reform established by Robert Lifton and the late Margaret Singer. Lifton's Eight Criteria for Thought Reform are: 1. Milieu Control; 2. Mystical Manipulation (Planned Spontaneity); 3. The Demand for Purity; 4. Confession; 5. Sacred Science; 6. Loading the Language; 7. Doctrine Over Person; and 8. Dispensing of Existence.[13] Briefly, it means coercive groups are a fantasy world of mystical manipulation, in which every sign points to the guru's version of truth.

Dispensing of existence means insiders discount non-members' and ex-members' basic dignity as souls. Gina explained,

> Those who have not learned TM are considered to live lives of ignorance. To have a life in ignorance is akin to a fate worse than death. Many TM devotees and youth, including myself decades ago, fear to live outside their global community's protected shell. They cannot meaningfully connect with outsiders. Leaving the TM movement to live on the outside was one of the more difficult decisions and processes of my life. It took years for me to develop meaningful relationships with non-meditators. I certainly stumbled in the process!

Gina bears a sense of responsibility toward the younger TM children as well as to her own children for their upbringing. She must deal with her own survivor's guilt because Gina and other observers fear conditions have worsened for TM children in recent years. She calls the current boarding schools, Maharishi ideal girls' schools, "structured environments of indoctrination." TM youth abuse alcohol and other substances in the communities and rebel with other self-destructive behaviors. Most of the youth eventually leave the community.

Besides the problems Gina sees in TM schools, she notes that adults who join authoritarian groups are often psychological adolescents themselves because they remain dependent on guru parent figures while neglecting the needs of their own children. This can happen whether the group is isolated, like the groups associated with Jonestown or Waco, or if the group is situated in the middle of a large city. The children may even attend public schools and appear normal to their teachers. Children of cults miss critical developmental milestones and upon leaving the groups, need extra emotional support.

Recognizing that it can be frightening to survive alone in the outside world, Gina and her children open their home to the younger TM children they know who are now attempting to leave the group. Gina observes that the children who had more contact with the outside world during their developmental years are better able to integrate into the outside world and live responsible lives. She credits her high school years living with various relatives for her later ability to transition into mainstream society and obtain a degree of professional success. Like many former members, Gina puts pressure on herself to succeed and sees herself as further behind in her career than she would like because of her cult beginnings.

While helping me complete this book, Gina's father died. His passing came just about a year after the Maharishi died, so I asked Gina what that was like. She explained:

My father died in May 2009 after decades of needless pain. He used Maharishi's magical remedies and promises, avoiding medical care for many years. He

28

lived with crippling painful rheumatoid arthritis. Maharishi and his Ayurvedic doctors taught that Western medicine would bring on more stress and toxins to the body, so my naively trusting, but otherwise intelligent, father avoided medical care. To the end, my father believed that he must have been a terrible person in a past life to have been afflicted with such severe daily pain. He said that he prayed to be free of the punishment for whatever pain he'd afflicted upon others. He hoped that those unknown others were no longer in pain. The guilt of this belief system weighed heavily upon him.

After he died, I found my father's photocopied purchase order records for Maharishi *yagyas*, which were essentially magical prayer ceremonies. These *yagyas* are trademarked to Maharishi Vedic Education Development Corporation (MVED). The order form states that the *yagyas* cost from $1,000 to $50,000.

Our parents gave thousands upon thousands of dollars for *yagyas* and Ayur Ved treatments, rather than receiving appropriate medical care for his painful medical condition. That is in addition to the many thousands of dollars spent on advanced courses, sponsoring others' (tax deductible) course participation, teacher training, and Maharishi Universities. This hyper commitment to their brand of spirituality was in lieu of cultivating their professions or family relationships.

During a conversation with my mother only a few weeks prior to my father's death, she said, "Gina, I don't know why your father is being so negative, talking about death and saying good bye to everyone."

I responded, "Mom, he's finally accepted his mortality. Dad is dying even though he meditated for nearly fifty years. He is ninety now and sick. The sooner you acknowledge his inevitable death, the better you'll be able to adjust when it happens."

How could anyone believe that paying thousands of

dollars for a mystical *yagya* would solve their life problems?[14]

Gina co-moderates a group blog with other former TM teachers. They maintain the site as a resource for recovery and insider information on the Transcendental Meditation organizations (tmfree.blogspot.com). She also maintains a personal blog that addresses cult recovery and other topics (comingtolifestories.com). Gina continues to untangle the webs that TM wove around her life. She stands by her mother as a loyal friend.

Harsh Remnants of My Childhood: The Hare Krishna Movement's Abuse of a Generation

Ananda

Ananda was born in 1975 and raised in the International Society for Krishna Consciousness, ISKCON, the Hare Krishna movement. As a child, she suffered neglect, as well as physical, sexual, and psychological abuse in the ISKCON boarding school in Dallas. She was a plaintiff in *Children of ISKCON vs. ISKCON* and a spokesperson to the media.

When Ananda was ten her parents withdrew her from the school and moved away from Dallas, but dysfunctional patterns continued to play out. Now in recovery, Ananda now lives, works, and raises her children away from ISKCON.

I met Ananda after we were both interviewed by the same

reporter in 2001.[15] We corresponded for several years, then I asked her to write her story for my research in 2004.

Group Profile and History

ISKCON is derived from a sect of Hinduism that originated in Bengal, India, in 1918. People in ISKCON trace the lineage back to earlier roots. Strict followers dress in traditional Hindu clothing and men shave their heads, leaving a tuft of hair as a ponytail (called a *sikha*) in the back. In the 1960s and 1970s, Hare Krishnas were known for their colorful chanting and dancing performances on city streets, and their hardcore fundraising activities in airports. Temple ceremonies attract Hindus to join the congregation and the organization holds what they call the Sunday feast at all their centers to welcome members of the public to a free meal. The group preaches vegetarianism, sobriety, and celibacy, and claims a worldwide following of millions of members.[16]

ISKCON's Founder-*Acharya* [original guru] A.C. Bhaktivedanta Swami Prabhupada first traveled to America in 1965 on a steam freighter to start the worldwide organization. His success opening temples all over the world was the fulfillment of his vision. Unfortunately, along with the good people who joined, criminal elements ensconced themselves in the hierarchy. There was a controversy over whether the criminal elements conspired to murder Prabhupada in 1977. The matter was never fully resolved, but most people in the organization do not believe it. Nevertheless, Prabhupada's death led to drastic changes in the organization.

To fill the leadership void, the Governing Body Commission (GBC), ISKCON's board of directors, promoted eleven disciples to be zonal *acharyas*, zonal gurus. These gurus reigned over their zones, and initiated their own disciples. Unfortunately, within the first ten years, nearly half of them left the organization over issues like drug smuggling, arms dealing, money laundering, assault, murder, or child abuse. In *Betrayal of the Spirit* and other writings, I explain the history in full.[17]

Ananda's Childhood

Ananda's parents put her in the Dallas boarding school as a child. She recalled:

> As a six-year-old child, from the moment I woke up at 3:30 in the morning, my world revolved around a deity, a statue, a figment of my imagination. I cowered and covered myself as I showered, ashamed of my nakedness. Krishna was all-powerful. He was always watching. To lust after a sweet, I punished myself with extra rounds of chanting. Though I carried an independent streak, I was a good child. I lived in utter fear of living. My own thoughts tormented me as a child, though I now see them as perfectly normal.

She believed exactly what they wanted her to believe, so in that sense her thoughts were normal. Some children like Flore A. (in the first story) intuitively saw through group programming and never bought into it. Others, like Ananda, fully believed it. ISKCON officials made sure this was the case. Ananda said,

> The communities kept us so close. We were tightly guarded from any outside influences, taught that the world outside of our community was frightening and full of offenders. . . . The fear kept us in line, kept us from venturing into the unknown world beyond the community. What happened behind ISKCON's walls was unbearable, but as children we knew no different. What we did know was that the outside world was worse.

Deprived of love and affection, the children were more vulnerable to sexual predators. Ananda explained,

> While the adults desperately tried to follow the principles, it was the young children who suffered the consequences of such a ludicrous ideology. We were easy prey, and an almost willing outlet for the sexual predators that frequented ISKCON's communities. Just to be spoken to was heaven, to have playtime and interaction, no matter what kind, was wonderful. The lack of attention drove some of us to act out in desperation for even the negative attention. Others withdrew further and further into themselves. To see the empty shallow eyes of these children was heartbreaking. I myself was desperate for attention and determined to get it no matter what I had to do.
> I held no resentment for my parents somehow, though I yearned for my mother's touch and would dream up excuses to try to force her to come back to me. As a precocious juvenile, at eight years old, I jumped off the ashram roofs to attempt to break my legs, knowing that she would have to return for me if I were injured. I

only succeeded in spraining my knees and ankles, and although once it did get her to come to me, she left again after a quick trip to the local drug store for some Ben Gay and Ace bandages. Then the guilt would overwhelm me once more and I would throw myself into my chanting to prove to Lord Krishna that I was apologetic and worthy of his love.

When I started this research, I had a nightmare of desperate children jumping from rooftops to purposely hurt themselves. When Ananda wrote her story for me, I was saddened and shocked to learn it really happened. Like many abuse victims, Ananda recalled suffering severe symptoms. She said,

It wasn't long before I disassociated myself from my surroundings, as if I were in another world, only occasionally catching glimpses of what was going on around me. The guilt I felt as a child overwhelmed me to the point of self-loathing. I saw myself as a headless body, my mind hovering and dancing above me, taunting my indiscretions, and leaving me when it got too painful to be myself.

Ananda was victimized by both male and female pedophiles, and the abuse by adult female predators left Ananda confused about her gender identity, as she explained,

Men hurt me; they always had, but it was okay, they said they loved me. Women on the other hand had never so much as said they loved me; they had never used that as a pretense to get me to award them anything in return, but I could see it in their faces, feel it in their touches. Their wandering hands in the ashrams were never discussed, never approached as "abuse." To this day I harbor feelings of guilt for enjoying and desiring what I now know was abuse.

The confusion of sex, love, and sexuality follows me and haunts me, makes me bitter and afraid to confront myself. Once I understood homosexuality, I vehemently denied to myself that I could have ever enjoyed the touch of a woman, yet somewhere in the back of my head I always remembered it as non-penetrating, non-physical, more emotionally loving and tender, therefore more desirable than anything a man could ever do.

My own desire for a normal life is a twisted confusing battle in my head. I want the strong, protective arms of a male surrounding me, yet I yearn for the sensuous and gentle touch of a woman. Relationships remain somewhat superficial while I struggle with the idea of love, and the idea of being loved.

Most of the ISKCON child abuse involved men abusing boys, along with much less common but still occurring incidents of women abusing girls. Pedophiles are not classified as homosexual, per se, but only as having a tendency to abuse boys or girls. I counseled the survivors to read books from the psychology aisle of bookstores, in hopes they would learn modern thinking on human sexuality. It is ideal of a young person grows up unashamed, loving their own bodies, and accepting their human sexuality as normal. The first sexual experience ideally takes place when a person is old enough to choose for him or herself out of free will with a willing partner. However, that is not the way in child abuse. Abusers choose for their victims, taking away their victims' innocence by force.

Even though Ananda's parents left the organization in 1985, they neglected Ananda, leaving her to her own ten-year-old resources to resolve any psychological problems she may have developed due to abuse in ISKCON. As a teen, Ananda entered into a sexual relationship with an older man who was supposed to be her guardian. It was a difficult transition into mainstream life, including additional statutory rape and motherhood at age sixteen. Ananda walked the path of self-hatred and self-blame until she got into recovery as an adult.

The truth is hard to bear, but it is medicine for betrayal's pain. If Ananda could have had the opportunity to work with a qualified recovery counselor upon leaving ISKCON, she may have avoided her adolescent turmoil and her recovery could have started sooner. People may try to hide the truth to protect victims, but victims already know the truth. They have already endured that which is considered too taboo for verbal consideration. Saying nothing and doing nothing to help victims has proven thoroughly ineffective.

ISKCON Child Abuse Dynamics and History

People are curious about the mindset of cult parents. The ones I knew when I was in the group genuinely believed in the organization and trusted the schools to raise their children. The majority were baby boomers who grew up in typical middle class nuclear families in the 1950s and 1960s. They joined because they were searching for life's answers or an alternative way of life. During my research in 1996, I met an old friend whose son was severely abused. She told me she suffered chronic, debilitating guilt that broke up her marriage. There are no statistics available, and many couples stayed together, but the child abuse caused much suffering for the families that were affected.

The child abuse was well hidden. ISKCON dogma forbade criticism of the leadership, calling the leaders pure devotees. Such pure souls were above scrutiny, even if they were caught in a lie. Further, ISKCON dogma included a heavy dose of chauvinism and resentment toward children. Children were little more than expensive material attachments. To rid members of these attachments, all parents had to enroll their children in the organization's boarding schools once they reached the age of five. In those days, if someone refused to do it, they usually had to leave the organization. The schools were called *gurukula*, which was Sanskrit for guru-school. Teachers escorted youngsters in lines to and from the temple for the early morning services, while the rest of the day they kept them cloistered in the schoolhouses.

The year 1971 marked the beginning of institutional abuse and neglect when ISKCON established its first *gurukula* in Dallas. That is the school Ananda attended. Government officials in Texas shut the school down within two years, then ISKCON opened its boys' schools in India. They also opened schools across America and in other countries where they had centers. Western European schools were adequately funded and staffed, and were not abusive, according to reports from people who attended the schools. The Los Angeles school was also not systemically abusive. Los Angeles did have a problem in the community nursery school, but they contacted the authorities and helped apprehend and convict the perpetrators.

The first cohort of ISKCON children were born in the sixties and seventies, when ISKCON was getting started. The abuse took place between 1971 and 1990[18] in the boarding school in Dallas, boarding schools in India, and schools in American rural communities, especially New Vrindaban, West Virginia. Abuse spread beyond these locations, because like in the Catholic Church, ISKCON transferred abusers to new territories to avoid detection.

While the organization sent all teenage boys to the boarding schools in India, they pressed teenage girls into service in the kitchens and other domestic areas. Arranged marriages between minor-aged girls and adult men took place in West Virginia, Los Angeles, and other locations in the 1970s and 1980s. Girls as young as twelve were married off to older men, and like minor-aged brides in the polygamous Mormon groups (PMGs), ISKCON's underage brides reported isolation, rape, and physical abuse.[19] Hridayananda, one of the zonal gurus, defended the practice when it occasionally came up for scrutiny.

In certain communities, individual abusers preyed on children during religious festivals, when parents and caretakers were preoccupied. All child abuse was covered up unless the ISKCON people perceived the rapist to be an outsider, for example, a new recruit or a fringe member. The punishment for outsiders was to beat them and pull out their *sikha* (ponytail) like a partial scalping, then eject them from the property. The most notorious example of this took place in Denver in the early years; but it was still going on, at least in the West Virginia center, when I was doing my research for this study in 1996.[20]

From my experiences and all the research I did on ISKCON's problems, I can say with certainty the organization hit bottom in 1986. By that time, the responsible, older disciples within ISKCON had turned against the zonal gurus. Some of them sought to bring about a conclusion to the illegal activities, including the child abuse. The reformers met in New Vrindaban, West Virginia. However, the reform movement quickly imploded.

At that time, the leaders of New Vrindaban, felt it necessary to assassinate one of the leading critics of the New Vrindaban guru. Steven Bryant (Sulochan) was not an official in the organization, but a disaffected follower who threatened to go to the media with the community's secrets. Along with some of the reformers, he had been searching for evidence the zonal guru system was illegitimate.

During that time, the leadership of New Vrindaban commissioned Thomas Drescher (Tirtha), a New Vrindaban hit man, to travel to Los Angeles to spy on, and kill, Bryant. On the night of May 22, Drescher located Bryant in his travel van, parked for the night near the Los Angeles temple. He approached Bryant, who was sitting in his van at the driver's side window. Drescher told him to chant, then shot him point blank in the head.

Police arrested Drescher within five days on a previous warrant, based on tips from people familiar with the situation. Although the organization claimed that Drescher and Bryant were estranged former members, the media covered the death as member-on-member cult violence. Bryant's death dealt a dramatic blow to the budding guru reform movement, public image, and internal integrity. Instead of eliminating a critic, as the gurus may have hoped, the murder led to negative media coverage of the organization as a whole.

Another decisive incident in 1986 was when Ramesvara, the zonal guru for Los Angeles, resigned his position and left ISKCON over his inappropriate contact with a minor-aged *gurukula* girl. He was also under a cloud of suspicion for drug trafficking, allegations he helped facilitate Bryant's murder, and a 1977 murder in Newport Beach.[21] Ramesvara's abdication sent a chilling message to child abusers and other criminals in ISKCON who had taken organizational protection for granted.

The most shocking event of 1986 was when Dylan Hickey (aka Nirmal-chandra), son of ISKCON Education Minister Jagadish and *gurukula* headmistress Laxmimoni, broke his neck falling from a tree at the ISKCON rural community in Pennsylvania. ISKCON authorities sent him to the hospital over miles of dirt road in the back of a station wagon instead of paying to airlift him out. Left a quadriplegic from the ordeal, Dylan started to write his memoirs of life at the Dallas and India boarding schools.

Coincidentally in 1986, the last American boarding schools closed (except for one girl's school headed by Laxmimoni). Starting that year, American temples have maintained local *gurukula* day schools, so children could live at home with their families. The organization-wide mandatory boarding school requirement ended in 1986. The problem first came out in the open in 1987-1988 at international *gurukula* meetings. In 1990, the GBC passed a comprehensive resolution stating that all suspected child abuse must be reported to the authorities.[22]

Just when the GBC passed their resolution, the full extent of the abuse started to come out. In 1990, survivors published their stories and began organizing reunions. The essay that resoundingly broke the silence about *gurukula* abuse was *Children of the Ashram*, by Raghunatha Anudas.[23] He started out writing a letter to a friend, but ended up with a twenty page essay about his history in the Dallas and India boarding schools. He published it in his own ISKCON Youth Veterans newsletter and mailed copies to all the ISKCON leaders, as well as to a list of *gurukula* survivors.

Raghunatha was one of the reunion organizers and put a tremendous amount of work into networking with the survivors. He helped organize *gurukula* reunions every year in Los Angeles in the 1990s, publishing his own newsletters, and taking part in other survivors' publishing efforts. Despite the work of Raghunatha and a core group of several dozen activist survivors, it still took six more years for the ISKCON leadership to acknowledge the harm to the abuse survivors. They finally acknowledged it at a 1996 regional GBC meeting in Florida[24] However, in the meantime, almost everyone else could see it. This raised the question of whether the leadership failed to see because they were slow to comprehend or because they did not want to see.

While that was going on, the Internet opened up to the public. Dylan Hickey and another survivor published a Website called V.O.I.C.E., Violations of ISKCON Children Exposed.[25] The site included survivor stories recounting the abuse and editorials about the organization's part in perpetuating and covering up the crimes.

In 1998, Dr. Burke Rochford, a sociology professor from Middlebury College, wrote an academic paper to document the history of child abuse, and the *ISKCON Communications Journal* published it.[26] The ISKCON Communications Office and Children of Krishna, Inc., sent out press releases, and *The New York Times*, Associated Press, Religious News Service, and newspapers across India printed stories with headlines like, "Hare Krishnas lift the lid on history of child abuse."[27]

After trying to find relief from the organization for two more years, in 2000, approximately one hundred petitioners filed a legal complaint, *Children of ISKCON vs. ISKCON*. ISKCON immediately entered bankruptcy protection. The bankruptcy courts required ISKCON to place notifications on the Internet and in various publications, and as a result, four hundred additional claimants joined the bankruptcy.

In May 2005, ISKCON filed a reorganization plan to settle with their victims. The case progressed slowly. One of the complications was that to receive part of the settlement, plaintiffs and claimants had to prove the degree of their abuse.[28] This procedure seems to be standard practice now, as the $668 million Los Angeles Roman Catholic Church settlement in June 2007 said that compensation to victims "will vary according to the severity of each case."

Plaintiffs and claimants obediently submitted layers of paperwork to bankruptcy attorneys for three years (2002-2005). Finally, in October 2008, the claims were settled, with ISKCON paying out millions of dollars to five hundred victims. Based on my research, There were an additional four or five hundred victims who chose not to join, or were unaware of, the lawsuit and bankruptcy.

Overall, ISKCON perpetrated systemic abuse and neglect for fifteen years (1971-1986), denied the harm it caused for another ten years (1986-1996), then took an additional twelve years to make peace with the victims (1996-2008). That is thirty-seven years, a lifetime for members of the abused generation who are now in their forties. Plus, there is reason to believe individual perpetrators still frequent the temples, and some schools in India still perpetrate systemic abuse.[29]

In ISKCON today, the boarding schools in the U.S. are shut down and temples have their own schools so the children can live at home.

There are pockets of reformers trying to change the organization from within and without. All along, there were individuals in the temples who wanted to do right by the *gurukula* victims. However, it took a lawsuit to force the organization to act.

Since 1977, when Prabhupada died, hundreds of splinter groups and non-affiliated Krishna consciousness groups have started. One researcher, Michael Gressett, Ph.D., a disciple of ISKCON, proposed in his dissertation there is a greater Hare Krishna movement. In America, he said, it may have started within ISKCON, but now it transcends the boundaries of the original organization. Like the original Christian church, hundreds, if not thousands, of new groups will spring from the old one, while the old one continues on.[30] No matter how the organization spreads and changes, the children's victory in *Children of ISKCON vs. ISKCON* stands as an urgent, vivid "no" followed by an exclamation point at the end of the ISKCON boarding-school experiment.

Loving an Abusive Reality:
Life as a Student of Aesthetic Realism
Ann S., M.A., M.Phil.

Ann S. was born into Aesthetic Realism in 1944, after her parents had been in the group for several years. Ann's mother founded an art gallery in 1955, so Ann grew up in the exciting and volatile art world of New York City. She and her parents were in the inner circle of the movement; Ann remained in the organization until age forty-one. She graduated from Brooklyn College summa cum laude and Phi Beta Kappa in 1965, and earned graduate degrees in Latin from Columbia University.

Living outside of the organization since 1985, Ann recently became an editor for *ICSA Today*, one of ICSA's new publications. We met in July 2010 at the final night dinner of the ICSA conference in New Jersey, and subsequently she agreed to participate in my study.

Group Profile

Aesthetic Realism revolved around founder Eli Siegel (1902-1978), a figure at the heart of the Greenwich Village scene of the mid-twentieth century. Siegel gained notoriety in 1920 when he won a coveted award from *The Nation* magazine for his poem, "Hot Afternoons Have Been in Montana." Following this success, he became the master of ceremonies for poetry readings at the Village Vanguard nightclub through the 1930s. He was one of the first Village poets to add jazz to poetry readings. He wrote for *Scribner's* and the *New York Evening Post Literary Review*.

In 1938 Siegel began teaching poetry. Then, in the early 1940s, he began giving poetry readings in his home, attracting a crowd of poets and artists. In 1941 he started to give individual sessions, engaging devoted followers like Ann's parents. In 1946, while giving weekly lectures at Steinway Hall, Siegel solidified his teachings into what he first called Aesthetic Analysis. He gradually gathered his writings into chapters of a book he called *Self and World: An Explanation of Aesthetic Realism*, which his followers published after his death. Although Aesthetic Realism is a psychology group, and not a religion, students consider Siegel's philosophy more profound than any religion.

Siegel's Aesthetic Realism has three principles: 1) "the deepest desire of every person is to like the world on an honest or accurate basis"; 2) "the greatest danger for a person is to have contempt for the world and what is in it"; and 3) "all beauty is a making one of opposites, and the making one of opposites is what we are going after in ourselves."[31]

Ann S.'s History in the Group

When Ann was born, her father was stationed on a troop carrier off Normandy, about to fight in one of the fiercest battles of World War II. Unlike many others in that battle, her father came home in 1945 when the war ended. Upon his return to America, he later told Ann, he first reunited with Eli Siegel, before going home to see his wife and baby.

Ann's parents raised her in the organization during its earliest days. Like Gina C.'s experience in Transcendental Meditation, Ann grew up as genetic royalty. She does not recall her earliest experiences, but said her mother would bring her as a baby to sessions with Siegel. Soon, the family moved into an AR group home, then ultimately to a brownstone in Manhattan walking distance to Siegel's place on Jane Street. Ann's family shared the property with ten other adults.

Growing up, Ann learned to revere Eli Siegel, just like everyone else around her. She recalled:

I believed Siegel's explanation that whatever problem I had—in life, at school, with friends—the reason was that I did not like myself because I was ungrateful to him.

She remembers Siegel's earnest side and times when he shared useful philosophical insights. Growing up, she admired his ideals. She heard him speak about literature, history, and politics. He could be charming and funny. However, she knew another side to him. She said, "I remember from the earliest time that Eli Siegel was like two people." She said his dark side was his emotional neediness. She recalled,

We would sit, thirty or so people, listening to him tell us how much good he had done our lives, and how we would never be happy until we acknowledged our debt of gratitude to him to the entire world. I would sit as far to the back of the room as possible, tears of shame running down my face, bending my head down behind the person in front of me so I wouldn't be called on to speak, and vowing inwardly to be honest from now on.

Former AR members say there was a strong distinction between inside and outside, and they considered outsiders inferior. Further, outsiders were enemies. Being around outsiders was considered an invitation to weakness and a reason to suspect a student's loyalty. Foundation employees rarely went anywhere. They considered their work to be the most important aspect of their lives and were reluctant to visit family or leave the group for any reason. Insiders felt an obligation to prove their great undying love, respect, and loyalty to Eli Siegel, AR, and, after Siegel's death, to the new leaders on a daily basis. They felt their loyalty to these objects of devotion must take precedence over all else in the world.

The inner circle consisted of as many as a hundred people at any given time, and, in Ann's opinion, it was a world of manipulation, peer pressure, emotional abuse, infighting, competition, cruelty, and isolation. It had a rigid hierarchy and people knew where they stood in it. Ann S. identified herself as part of a "second tier, who acted as the henchmen for this leadership."

Insiders could only associate with their non-cult family if the family members demonstrated admiration for the group, such as offering praise or donations. If group leaders perceived a student's outside family members as antagonistic (or not sufficiently enthusiastic), the leaders discouraged the connection. One ex-member said:

> They were not told directly that they could not see their family, but the pressure not to was so great that very few students had the fortitude to buck the tide and do it anyway. . . . A student could gain status in the group by completely renouncing and shunning non-cult family members.

Ann recalled when her mother did not visit her dying father (Ann's grandfather), Siegel said her mother showed what he called "the new kindness." This implied that dedication to him and demonstrating disapproval of her father's attitude to Aesthetic Realism were the criteria for kindness.

The worst punishment within the inner circle was to become a student in disfavor. The leaders held weekly meetings to single out and verbally abuse fallen members. Anyone who held back from heaping on verbal abuse could also be suspect. After these drubbings, everyone shunned the students who fell from grace. Eventually, the leadership would forgive students and welcome them back into grace.

Even though the doctrine officially preached contempt for the world was bad, members were encouraged to feel justified contempt towards those outside the group who did not know or agree with their philosophy, and towards fellow members who had fallen from grace or left.

Ann recalled Siegel's rage if he perceived resistance in a student or when people failed to acknowledge what an important person he was. She recalled:

> He believed *The New York Times* refused to write about
> him because reporters and editors didn't want to learn
> from him. He believed the art world boycotted him
> because he explained beauty and they could not. He
> believed what he taught could end war, racism, poverty,
> and crime; and that he was singled out for hatred
> because he knew more than the authorities in every
> field.

Ann's mother opened the art gallery in 1955, and devoted all her
time to her work, making it the center of the family's life. At that
time, Ann entered the seventh grade at Hunter High School in
Manhattan. She had a best friend at school who envied her bohemian
communal lifestyle, but Ann envied the other children's lives. She
recalled:

> My school friends had busy homes, visited relatives,
> traveled—and they did not have to go to sessions and
> hear criticism of their contempt. Siegel said I was a
> snob, using my intellectual Hunter girlfriends against
> him. If I were honest, he said, I would be telling my
> friends about him.

Siegel started a poetry class for the children of AR and Ann
brought her best friend to these classes. She recalled that her friend
liked the classes at first, but stopped attending after she felt pressure
to become an advocate for Eli Siegel. When her friend showed
resistance, Ann cut off her relationship.

Living in the brownstone, Ann started to feel a special sense of
responsibility to make the world aware of Eli Siegel. She said, "I
remember sitting on the floor in a room full of adults, wondering
why I alone of all the children I knew had to take part in such a
discussion."

In college, Ann was a zealous advocate for Eli Siegel and AR. She spoke to classmates about AR and turned in papers laced with AR philosophy, earning good grades. She even attracted media attention, and gave newspaper interviews about AR. Ann grew up as a model child within the group, a demonstration of what AR could do. However, in the mid-1960s when she won a graduate fellowship to Columbia University, and was excited about going there, Siegel accused her of using Columbia University to feel superior to him. He said she had "architectural snobbishness," comparing the grand buildings on the Columbia campus to the modest surroundings of AR. She recalled being torn between guilt for betraying Eli Siegel and her desire to pursue her graduate education:

> I became terribly anxious, and took to my bed. I cried for hours. I would not talk to anyone. Only my mother's coaxing and finally a telephone call from Mr. Siegel got me back in circulation. I went to graduate school, but my grades fell, I was ill at ease on campus, and ultimately, though I earned a masters degree and completed all the exams for a Ph.D., I gave up academics to teach Aesthetic Realism.

In 1971, Siegel named some of his students, including Ann and her parents, as teachers. Then in 1974, Ann's mother persuaded Siegel to let his followers buy a building in Soho to start an Aesthetic Realism school, and the Aesthetic Realism Foundation took shape. Ann became a leader, directing public programs, helping students write their papers, and preparing the application to become a non-profit foundation. However, Ann felt like a phony. She recalled:

> I was admired because I had studied so many years with Eli Siegel, but I rarely lived up to the person everyone expected me to be. There was a set of attitudes, to the press, one's family, other students, we had to adopt, replete with language we were expected to use. Even

when I used the right words, I did not convince myself,
and I was in constant expectation of the criticism, which
always came.

After the Foundation started, Siegel came down with a prostate
condition, but refused medical treatment. It became so bad he could
not walk, so he remained in his room. One of Siegel's students took
over teaching his classes, and Ann recalled: "We were all afraid to
call or visit, and secretly relieved we did not have to attend his
classes." When Siegel finally went for surgery, it was too late. In the
months leading up to his death, he lived in the home of one of his
students, and Ann was one of the people designated as a caregiver.

During this time, a female follower began talking about being
physically close to Siegel for many years, and claimed Siegel's wife
and the woman's husband knew of the arrangement and allowed it to
go on. This was a major disillusionment. Ann recalled:

I began to feel there was something crazy going on,
though I could not say this to anyone except my mother,
who confessed she agreed with me.

Also in the years before and just after Siegel's death, a few people
rose to power, people Siegel had praised for their ethical strength.
However, these new leaders instituted practices Ann had never
known Siegel to condone, such as interfering with people's
marriages. They ran the Aesthetic Realism Foundation at their whim.

Ann continued to support this leadership, because as she put it: "I,
too, thought I knew what was right for people better than they did
themselves." However, she said when she heard these leaders
secretly mock Eli Siegel, she started to see them as power hungry
and cruel. Soon, the new leaders accused Ann's mother of ethical and
financial impropriety and forced her out as the Foundation's director.
Although Ann's mother did not openly oppose the rebuke, Ann
believed it was false and unfair. She recalled:

My mother had sacrificed her painting career because
the art critics who praised her would not accept her
praise of Eli Siegel. I had watched her all the years I
grew up trying to measure up to Siegel's ethical criteria,
and internalizing his criticism to the point where she felt
she was responsible for his suffering. Now she was
accused of sabotaging his work.

This was the main event that made Ann question her commitment
to AR. In 1984, she resigned as an officer and took a part-time
typing job at a non-profit Jewish agency. She felt she led a double
life, working by day, then suffering verbal abuse at AR meetings in
the evenings. Over the next two years, she started to sense things
were fundamentally wrong with the group. Outside, people seemed
to accept her; inside they were rabidly critical. Outside, she could
freely date men; inside, people cautioned men to stay away from her
because she was unethical. Finally, she walked out.

Coincidentally, she left the same day as another student whom
she had briefly dated, but who had stopped asking her out because
other students warned him to stay away from her. Once outside, he
called her, they began dating again, and they soon married. They
have remained happily married since 1987. Ann's in-laws are
sympathetic to her history and accept her for who she is.   Ann's
father remained in the group until his death in 2009, and she does not
expect her mother, after seventy years, will leave. Because Ann left,
they cut her off. Ann said,

The exception was in 1998 when critical statements I
made about Aesthetic Realism were quoted in an article
in the *New York Post*, and I received a five-page
vitriolic letter, most likely written in committee, but
over my parents' signatures. It compared me to Brutus
assassinating Julius Caesar, and to Benedict Arnold.
When I pass former colleagues on the street, they look
past me as if I do not exist.

The organization continues as a non-profit educational foundation based in Soho that offers lectures, private consultations, and classes in poetry, anthropology, art, and music. They also have a theater company and the art gallery Ann's mother founded.

Dilemma of Children from Lesser Known Cults

If a child grows up in a well known religious cult like the Unification Church or Hare Krishans, there is de facto more reason to believe the group is a cult. However, in lesser known authoritarian groups, the cult question is up for debate. Aesthetic Realism is a perfect example. On its surface, the group appears benign. They have deep roots in the alternative East Village, including a school and art gallery. Even the teachings seem benign. As one ex-member said,

> It's not the teachings of Aesthetic Realism that cause some people to call AR a cult; most former members aren't critical of the AR philosophy itself.[32]

Ann left the group in 1985, but it took many years before she realized the group fit the description of a cult. She said as she approached her fiftieth birthday, she began to work with a therapist trained in cult recovery work. She said,

> My years of therapy helped me understand what the dynamic of my upbringing had in common with all families, which was extremely beneficial. I previously thought everything about my experience was unique, which was not entirely true. As a result, through therapy, I felt less different from other people.

Through therapy, Ann gradually acknowledged her group experience had cultic qualities. Around that time, her husband and others encouraged her to visit the Cult Hotline and Clinic in New York City. However, she vowed to stay away from cult recovery work, in part because it reminded her of the AR experience. She said,

> I didn't want to be anywhere near a group of any kind, and certainly not one that I feared would share the evangelical spirit I now scorned. I also felt, as much as cult educators understood, there was something in my experience they could not grasp. There was a wound that would not heal. I thought it was a weakness in me, something to be ashamed of not overcoming, and so I hardly ever talked about it even to people who had left my own movement.[33]

Then, in 2006, Ann accepted an invitation to attend an ICSA workshop for second generation adult ex-cult members[34] to be held in her home state. She said, "That workshop literally turned me a hundred and eighty degrees, and has impacted my life ever since."

Meeting others who shared the second generation experience was a milestone in Ann's recovery. She said,

> When an individual chooses to join a group, there is something to compare the group to, no matter how deeply buried; and there are usually friends and family in the outside world. When you are born into one, there is no other experience.
>
> When I walked into that room filled with people who shared that specific experience, being born to parents who already belonged to a movement, never knowing anything other than that environment from day one, I felt a connection I had not felt anywhere before, and a bond with those people I will never lose. Others may grasp intellectually what occurred, but there is an emotional level only one who has shared the experience understands. A door opened. It was a beginning point

for trust, for opening up inner areas of myself, to myself and also, however slowly, to the outside world.

Ann said she wants to add to people's understanding of the cult phenomenon and turn her painful experiences into something of value to the world. She said,

> AR represents the kind of outwardly benign, culturally dressed group that inwardly mangles people's minds.[35] That's the part that means the most to me. I'm lucky. I escaped because somehow my critical voice wouldn't die, but it hasn't been easy liberating it from all the garbage imposed on it over forty-one years. I still struggle with inherited views and limitations. The mental damage done by a dogma whose manipulations are so well disguised can be especially difficult to understand and undo.

Long Errand Out of the Labyrinth: A Childhood of Slavery in the Children of God

Jane Doe

Jane Doe was born into a group known as the Children of God in the early 1970s. As a child, the organization moved her around to more than a dozen locations in Latin American countries. Her childhood in the notoriously abusive group left her with physical and emotional damage.

Jane first contacted me by email in September 2004 to learn more about my research. We spoke on the phone and she agreed to tell me her life story for this book.

Group Profile

The term Jesus Freaks describes a subculture of alternative Christian groups in the 1960s and 1970s, and in its early days, the group known as the Children of God was the most visible.[36] The group claimed eighteen thousand followers at the cusp of the 1960s and 1970s, when it was one of the largest alternative Christian movements in the world. They believed their leader, born David Brandt Berg in 1919, was like a modern Moses. Nicknamed Mo, he would lead them through apocalyptic times beginning in 1974, when Comet Kohoutek would pass close to the earth.

Berg was born into a family of evangelical Christian preachers, including his parents and maternal grandfather. For a time, he was a minister in his father's church, the Christian and Missionary Alliance, but he was expelled. He traveled with his mother, wife, and teenaged children in a ministry they called Teens for Christ. Around 1968 this evolved into the group known as the Children of God. A local newspaper reporter called them by that name, and David Berg adopted it for a time. They also called themselves the Family, Family of Love, or Family International. At this time, the group seems to have disbanded and does not have a name. However, a following still exists for the late David Berg and his partner, Karen Zerby, aka Mama Maria. Maria's new partner, now second in command, is Steven Douglas Kelly, aka Peter Amsterdam, or King Peter.

Berg controlled his flock through dictations called the Mo Letters. Some materials were for a general audience, while others were top secret; followers had to read and burn the most secret communications. In 1974, Berg revealed the Law of Love,[37] which allowed sex between adults and minors, and between all members of the group. However, male homosexuality was strictly forbidden. The group followed what Berg called the one wife doctrine, which basically declared all adults in the group to be married. Berg also preached sexual abuse of children.

Jane's Childhood

Jane served her time in communes across South America, where she remembers forced labor, indoctrination, fundraising, and sexual abuse. She recalled:

> Having been indoctrinated from an early age that my body was not my own and that to withhold it was selfishness and a grave sin, I tried my best to be elsewhere in my head until it was over—for a time. It was confusing to think that I was wrong, as the cult's doctrine held, to have negative feelings about what those men did to me.

Jane remembers two police raids on Family communes in Latin America. In one case group members had to flee to a compound in the jungle; in the other, Jane lied to cover up abuse out of fear of retaliation from the adults. She also remembers the time David Berg reiterated his dogma that sex with anyone of any age was welcome. She remembers the sexual assaults she endured as a child growing up in group homes.

She remembers when the organization published *Liberty or Stumbling Block?* The 1986 statement by one of the group's officials,

Sara Davidito, an attempt to end the practice of sex with minors. It stated in part:

> Responsible, mature, of-age teens (of legal age) may be a different story, but for the record, we want to say that we do not agree with adults having sex with children. The Family should just not do it, mainly because it's illegal.[38]

While it would have been a logical improvement, Jane recalled that it did not stop all of the abusers.

Jane was sent to live in a teen training camp that taught teenage inmates to see themselves as foot soldiers in the end time army of the Family. The teens' lives were a permanent boot camp from that time until the anticipated apocalypse. The end was supposed to come in 1993, but in 1986 David Berg pushed it forward, crediting his own group for temporary grace from the inevitable. By this time, Jane had lost faith in Berg and his hallucinations.

In a number of communes where Jane lived, adults used children over the age of twelve for sex, and one place established schedules that assigned minors a partner and time slot for sharing. Sharing was their euphemism for sex.

Finally, as a teenager, Jane escaped the group and moved to the United States. She said:

> I have survived thus far, but some of my peers have been less fortunate. Many have perished. There have been suicides and other deaths resulting from overdoses. Upon leaving the group, some have ended up in the sex trade due to lack of skills, education, or family support.

Long Road of Denial

After some years, Berg decreed that the best way to indoctrinate outsiders, which he called sheep, was to attract them with sex. He called this flirty fishing, or ff-ing, and ordered women in the group to arrange call girl-like relationships with men, referred to in the group as fish. Male benefactors who could donate money and provisions, and do other favors for the group, were called kings. In some cases, men also ff'ed women. It was an obvious sign something was seriously wrong, but the disciples who stayed with Berg either refused to see it, or thought things would soon change for the better.

In her autobiography, *Heaven's Harlots: My Fifteen Years as a Sacred Prostitute in the Children of God,*[39] Miriam Williams explained how she adapted:

> When I first joined, the group was very puritanical with strict rules about separating boys and girls. Now we shared sexually, not only within our group, but also with the lost souls outside. We witnessed by practicing self-sacrificial love including laying down our lives and our bodies. Only the dedicated stayed through this transition from Jesus People to radical "fishers of men." I was one of those who stayed, convinced that whatever was done for love could not be wrong. But now, I was doing it for money.[40]

Berg forbade birth control, so female followers had multiple children. Miriam Williams had five before she finally left the group. Children born of ff'ing unions were called Jesus Babies, because they were, as Williams put it, "like Jesus ... born to mothers whose fathers were unknown [sic]." Further, members and their children were photographed for child pornography.[41]

Allegations against the late David Berg and his followers include incest, polygamy, prostitution, and child pornography. Berg was a child abuse victim and self-admitted alcoholic, and after the death of his overbearing mother Virginia Berg in 1968, all his formerly repressed sexuality burst forth in the bizarre sexual ideology he taught his followers.[42]

People often ask me why somebody doesn't do something about

abusive groups like the one David Berg started. I have thought about this quite a bit, especially in the past few years while working on this project. For one thing, people are trying, and we do succeed in getting justice for some victims. However, corrupt gurus are many and resources are scarce. Plus, it is difficult to investigate an isolated group's inner workings.

The victims of David Berg want to initiate a lawsuit, but the group has always done its best to hide its assets and leadership, and recently has taken steps to appear to cease to exist. Suing the individuals involved would be costly and would probably not bring monetary awards. Thus, any definitive lawsuits against the group remain stalled.

One advantage of lawsuits is they bring the victims' stories to light. There are other ways to get the truth out, but lawsuits levy allegations and force the defendants into action. Arresting perpetrators would do the same thing, but jurisdictional issues and statutes of limitation may prevent prosecution. There are ways to work around this in some cases. Judges may rule that the time limit started once the victims realized what happened to them was unlawful, rather than when the acts actually occurred.

David Berg is a striking example of a destructive leader. He exerted total control over his disciples that led to ruthless exploitation of children. It is hard to imagine how parents in the group could accept David Berg's twisted teachings.

Berg is dead and the heirs to his legacy have tried to distance themselves and disavow any wrongdoing. With no help in sight, victims may take things into their own hands. Acting out years of repressed anger, they may try to hurt the abusers or people who covered up the abuse. Perhaps if there had been any other way to shine a light on the history, then Ricky Rodriguez would not have resorted to murder and suicide.

Ricky was the son of Maria David, David Berg's partner. Ricky was born of a flirty fishing encounter, but David Berg accepted Ricky as his own son. The Bergs proclaimed that Ricky, known as Davidito in the group, would lead the followers during the end times. They called their son the prince and set him up as an example for all the other children. They produced a 762 page book referred to as the *Davidito Book* which was intended to be a parenting manual for group members, including instructions on how to sexualize children.

The book had photographs of Ricky being sexually molested.

Group spokespersons claimed Ricky had survived emotionally intact and his upbringing had not harmed him. Then on January 9, 2005, he called one of his childhood caregivers, Angela Smith, to his Tucson, Arizona, apartment and stabbed her to death. He then drove 260 miles to the isolated town of Blythe, California, where he shot himself in the head. Ricky left behind a video he taped just before the murder. In it, he spoke about his emotional pain over child exploitation in the group. As he loaded his gun in full view of the camera, he listed the different means he had considered for suicide. In the video Ricky explained,

I'm not gonna sit here and say—oh yeah, I had it the worst—or I didn't—because it really doesn't matter. It should never have happened at all. To anybody. That's the point. So that's when I started contemplating suicide.[43]

He criticized his mother, her partner, and the current leaders, and imagined how they would feel if

somebody went into their house, or their f-ing motor home, or whatever, and poured gasoline on them, then lit a match, and had a f-ing barbecue. It would be like—wow—there is justice in this world. . . . And an incredible weight would be lifted off my shoulders. And I would be able to go on with my life. Yeah, I would have f-ing problems, but I got stuck on this one thing. I got stuck because there's this need that I have. This need—it's not a want. It's an f-ing need. And I wish it wasn't, but it is. It's a need for revenge. It's a need for justice. Because I can't go on like this.[44]

Major media reported the murder-suicide, exposing the abuse Ricky and others wanted the world to acknowledge. In 2007, the

Cinemax TV network aired a documentary by another victim of the Children of God, Noah Thomson.[45] *Los Angeles Times* staff writer Mary McNamara wrote in her review,

> If Ricky Rodriguez had not committed a murder-suicide two years ago, *Children of God: Lost and Found* would probably not have wound up on Cinemax. . . . Mainly because Rodriguez left videotape explaining his actions: as the victim of repeated sexual abuse in the name of The Family, he was bent on getting what revenge he could.[46]

The documentary showed that adult group members are still unapologetic and deep in denial. As the *L.A. Times* reviewer pointed out:

> [The filmmaker's own mother] refuses to believe any of it, including her own son's experiences. Over several phone conversations, she speaks in the polite but firm voice of a customer sales representative, repeatedly refusing to participate in the documentary.[47]

This event deeply affected my subject, Jane Doe, and all of the first cohort of children in this group. I include details about Ricky because his life and death, and the murder he committed, are a common story they all shared, including attending the memorial. Ricky's act brought the group's story of abuse out in the open once and for all. However, it's tragic it had to come to that end. Perhaps the survivors express it best. A post on the ex-Family Website, movingon.org, said:

> I am still trying to come to grips with what Ricky did. I am also trying to come to grips with what happened to Ricky growing up and the unfathomable

pain it obviously left him with. And with the variations on the *Davidito Book* brand of childcare that trickled down to my own childhood in Family Homes, scarring my life. I have wracking grief over my childhood and that of my siblings and friends. . . .

I attended the memorial in the hope that there will be no more Rickys, starting with no more childhoods like his and no more lies. I do not pray; my attendance was as close as I can bring myself to a prayer. It would be a step in the right direction if The Family's leadership would acknowledge the extent of the damage and take actions to remedy it.

When will people learn the disastrous effects of trying to smother another's will with your own? This mother's day I will pause to think of the mother that abandoned me in favor of Ricky's mother, and to acknowledge how sorrowful I am for Ricky that he had the mother he did.[48]

Many worthy and lovable children unfortunately came into this world through coercive cult practices. In this group it was casual sex; in other groups it was leaders telling women whom to sleep with or marry. But even children born into nuclear families were often taken away from their homes to grow up as wards of the group. Taking children away from their parents is a red flag for child abuse. Juliana Buhring, one of the authors of a shocking memoir about Children of God, *Not Without My Sister*,[49] describes the pain she and her peers felt growing up:

The philosophy of the group was to take children away from backslider parents and hand them over to The Family. Some children had been separated for years— and some never saw their parents again and had no idea where they were because their names had been changed.[50]

Backslider is the trigger word for shame heaped on members who are not fully committed. In the following passage, an adult raised in the group reminds us that anger is a natural stage for victims on the way to getting back their souls:

> One of the basic needs of a young person leaving a cult is permission to be angry. . . . It is vital to me now to have a sense of control over my life and to feel that I have a say and can actually do what I choose.[51]

Finally feeling angry at the perpetrator(s) is a positive breakthrough. It is a sign the ex-member is ready to grasp what the group experience was all about. Premature forgiveness could smother the little spark of awakening. Quick forgiveness only serves to excuse the perpetrators.[52]

Another issue for ex-members is whether to confront the guru(s), cult parents, or other cult members. It is a complex question, similar to confronting an incest perpetrator. Recovery expert John W. Wilson said of confrontation:

> For some people it is a logical step in their recovery; for others it could be a dangerous and self-destructive act. The real meaning of confrontation is to stand up to the abuse. It represents a recognition that:
> • What happened to the client was abusive.
> • Sexual child abuse is wrong.
> • The client did not deserve to be abused.
> • The client is not responsible for the abuse.
> • People must be accountable for their actions.[53]

In reality, there may be no way to talk things out with members of a coercive group. It may be as fruitless as trying to have a rational discussion with a practicing addict. David Berg's institutionalization of broken sexual boundaries, guilt, neglect, and hyper-discipline left an estimated one thousand young people emotionally scarred. I include this story to show one of the most striking examples of child abuse in a closed group.

Conclusion:

Deescalating the Cult Dynamic in Society

Although the media uses the word cult to describe closed groups like the ones I write about, the word "cult" is taboo in academic circles. They consider it unhelpful because it is pejorative. Academics generally need to stay on good terms with the groups they study, and judgmental name-calling does nothing to improve relations.

The study of the dangerous cult phenomenon began as early as 1936, when the world of psychology recognized a syndrome called identification with the aggressor[54] This means, due to unfulfilled emotional needs, victims may cling to their abuser(s) for validation and acceptance. In refusing to acknowledge the danger an aggressor poses, victims trust the aggressor and think the real danger comes from the outside world. A similar thing happens in abusive relationships, and is called battered wife syndrome.

Stockholm syndrome is another name for it that dates back to a 1973 bank robbery in Stockholm. The robbers held employees hostage for six days and won them over. By the time the ordeal ended, the employees were defending their captors.

Most people recall the Hearst kidnapping in 1974, another classic example of Stockholm Syndrome. A group that called itself the Symbionese Liberation Army kidnapped nineteen-year-old Patricia Hearst. She was the heiress of the late newspaper publisher William Randolph Hearst. In captivity, Patty Hearst joined the militants in robbing banks, and was ultimately arrested and sent to prison. Security cameras caught her brandishing an M1 Carbine semi-automatic rifle, a photo that came to symbolize identification with the aggressor.

A related term is authoritarianism, which was used to describe fascism and Nazism during World War II. Brainwashing is another term, which most solidly applied to Korean treatment of prisoners of war during the Korean War. *Snapping: America's Epidemic of Sudden Personality Change*, by Flo Conway and Jim Siegelman (1978), boosted the word snapping into the discussion.

Margaret Singer, Ph.D. (1921-2003), and Robert Lifton, M.D., led the study of coercive group behavior from the 1960s on. Dr. Singer called it mind control, and served as an expert witness in the Hearst trial and other cases. Dr. Lifton's *Eight Criteria for Thought Reform*[55] is the definitive description of a coercive system.

Identification with the aggressor, brainwashing, snapping, mind control, and thought reform all hint at the same thing. However, after

67

nearly eighty years of research, nobody, including the American Psychiatric Association, can come up with a good name for it.[56] But what better way to solve a problem, than to agree on what to call it?

One reason for the resistance is that if we called a dangerous cult a cult, and calling brainwashing what it is, then we would have to acknowledge that cults and brainwashing can take hold in all our social institutions: families, religion, media, the workplace, and governments.

Acknowledging the dark side of our institutions seems dangerous, but if we want to protect children, we must recognize the trust bandits[57] and confidence tricksters[58] for the criminals they are. Alice Miller, a German analyst who grew up in Nazi Germany, and who has written extensively on child abuse recovery, said:

> We can no longer afford to deny our perceptions and evade the truth, even if it is painful, for only the truth can save us.[59]

Preventing Child Abuse

Since child abuse can easily take root in a closed system, it is tragic parents try to protect children by repeating the warning, "Do not talk to strangers." Although parents need to educate their children about kidnappers, pedophiles, and the like, shunning all outsiders is the wrong answer. If children are already isolated, telling them not to talk to strangers just puts them in more danger. Most child abuse perpetrators are known to the family, or members of the family.

One program, widely advertised on television in the early 00s, sought to prevent child abuse by limiting the time children spend with adults. They call this strategy "minimize opportunity." They say the most dangerous scenario is a "one-adult/one-child situation." To avoid temptation, they recommended adults never be alone with a child other than their own.[60]

I believe this is an overreaction because only a small percentage of adults are pedophiles. Most adults respect generational boundaries and simply do not see children as sex objects. It is paranoid to treat all adults as potential abusers.

You can prevent sexual abuse for your own children if you speak frankly with them and offer age-appropriate advice. For example, an age old adage is to ask them to tell you or another trustworthy adult if anyone tries to touch them in the areas their bathing suits cover. This is non-threatening and easy for a child to understand.

Healing for Victims

Most children born or raised in dangerous cults leave their groups in their late teens or mid-twenties, and tens of thousands enter mainstream society each year.[61] The extent of abuse, and whether the person blames him or herself, determines the prognosis for recovery.

Unhealed victims may feel no one listens to them. They may tell bits and pieces of their story indiscriminately to everyone they meet, including acquaintances and strangers. This turns people off, isolating and invalidating victims even more. Everyone needs a healthy emotional boundary there:

> Consider another person's level of interest and caring before opening up to them. Choose the right time and place to discuss your personal issues.

My way to hear victims is through their writing, because it is a creative process they can do at their own pace. Artwork is another good way to process memories. One of my teachers, art therapist Dr.

Janie Rhyne, explained how to use art for healing. She said:

> I find that some of us can use fantasy as a way of
> finding reality. Art experience can offer a way for you
> to try this, and the art form you create can provide you
> with a means of interpretation and a potential for
> transformation. . . . Empty out [the fantasy world] area
> and look at its contents.[62]

Prior to Gestalt, Humanist, and Jungian art therapists, the world
of art therapy was based on Freudian theory. Sigmund Freud (1856-
1939) was an Austrian doctor who founded psychoanalysis. He said
all human emotional problems hinged on sexual guilt. He used art
therapy, but only to look for symbols that may point to a patient's
guilty sexual feelings. Rhyne rejected Freud's theory, stating she
would never attempt to read in something sexual that may not
actually be there. Rather, she teaches people to see the holistic
reality represented in their art piece.

Gestalt therapists are trained to listen for significant metaphors in
their clients' words, dreams, writing, and artwork. They then amplify
the symbols for the client. Gestalt therapist Barry Stevens (1902-
1985) related a story of how she led a client to explore a significant
symbol from a dream.

> A girl told her dream . . . . which began in some fields.
> Then she moved on, and came to a bridge. That was the
> end of the dream. She didn't cross the bridge. . . . She
> wanted to start with the fields, and this felt right to me.
> After that, she wanted to go somewhere else in her
> dream. I asked her to go to the bridge . . . That the
> bridge took her on a journey from which she got an
> existential message is not strange.[63]

The client could have easily forgotten the bridge, and not gotten
back to it. Luckily, Barry Stevens noticed it and invited the client

back to explore it and imagine what was on the other side. This led to what Barry Stevens calls an existential message. Nowadays we might call that a realization, connecting the dots, finding peace of mind, or achieving clarity.

Symbols encapsulate the message of growing up in a dangerous cult. Think back to the vivid images the writers in this book shared from their childhoods: Flore remembers the musicians in the train station, singing to her to try to mitigate her tears on the worst day of her childhood. Gina remembers her initiation day when she realized the initiator had given all the children the same mantra. Ananda remembers jumping from the roof to try to get her mother to stop her cult activities and pay attention to her. Ann remembers having to cater to the tremendous ego of her group's leader, and losing her best friend who could not do the same. Jane remembers the force labor, indoctrination, and having to lie to the authorities about the sexual abuse that was rampant in the group. These images are real memories for these individuals, but also stand as symbols, metaphors, for the pain of growing up in a demanding cultic group.

Those who do not study dangerous cults may think the problem has gone away. It is true, most of the old groups are still around, but less visible than before. People recognize the big names and know better to stay away. But there are many smaller, lesser known groups, that can turn just as abusive. Many are Christian, or purport to be Christian.

There was a cultish Christian group uncovered on the campus of the University of Arizona recently. Although the group had been recruiting members on campus for twenty-five years, the University revoked their membership immediately when the dark side of Faith Christian came to light.[64]

Faith Christian allegedly got students to change their majors and go to work for the church after they graduated. In the area of child abuse, the Faith Christians allegedly taught followers to hit infants with a cardboard tube when they tried to lift their heads up in the crib. Members believed children needed to be controlled like this from birth or they would grow up defiant. They also hit babies with wooden spoons, hard enough to leave a mark in the shape of a spoon.

People might be unaware that a seemingly nice little Christian group could operate like a dangerous cult and abuse children. But dangerous cult leaders can take any philosophy and turn it into a poison and attract followers. Another break with the past is that we now have the threat of cult-like groups that encourage followers to commit terrorism. Spreading knowledge about the dangerous cult phenomenon is more important than ever.

Appendix I

Ten Traits of Groups that Tolerate Abuse

1. Immature, unqualified, and possibly psychologically damaged people work their way into positions of power. When it comes to leadership, the people at the nexus of power are usually either evil or stupid.

2. There's always more than one type of abuse taking place. While people in the system may feel a vague uneasiness or depression, people at the top could be involved in illegal activities that would put them in jail for a long time. Like the fable of the blind men and the elephant, everyone sees a different aspect of the problem.

3. Communication is choked with collective secrets, duplicity, deceit, gossip, and backstabbing. It's not okay to talk about feelings, or criticize the leaders for the abuses taking place. The bad

73

communication starts a cycle of verbal abuse, because people caught in these systems tend to become verbally abusive.

4. Although it seems paradoxical, the more rigid and controlling a system is, the more abuse it will tolerate. It works like this. On one hand you have incompetent leaders who are either covering up their mistakes, or working out devious plots to exploit a situation. While they are involved in their egotistical pursuits, they clamp down on everyone else to prevent suspicion.

5. Leaders demand absolute loyalty. The people at the center of an abusive system set themselves up as beyond reproach. Like all good psychopaths, they can be charismatic and work a room like they're running for office. They may portray themselves as pillars of the community, or pious and holy. But in their darker moments, they are a domineering force that nobody can cross.

6. People within an abusive system think they are superior to all outsiders. For example, in a dangerous religious cult, insiders may look down on outsiders as godless. In extreme cases, the insiders may see the whole outside world as their enemies. The same condescending "us and them" attitudes develop in most systems that tolerate abuse.

7. Life in an abusive system is a constant state of upheaval. The chaos is usually a result of bad leadership, and conveniently covers

up the follies of the leaders. The leaders keep everything moving at a fast pace, so followers lose track of what's really going on.

8. In an abusive system, people don't honor each others' boundaries. Even if there's no sexual exploitation taking place, victims of the system might feel drained at having to do what everyone else tells them to do, and inability to draw the line at how much they have to give. This leads to Stockholm Syndrome, which means the victims of the system actually believe the propaganda. They think sticking with the group is their only means of survival in a dark and cruel world.

9. Sexual exploitation is another trait of systems that tolerate abuse. The backdrop of chaos attracts rapists and pedophiles, and the whole system may be infested with dangerous predators of all kinds. The worst groups knowingly harbor criminals, and even bring them into the nexus of the group. Abusive leaders may purposely befriend people who are onto them, if only to keep them from going to the authorities. Due to the amount of sexual exploitation they cover up, all touching or shows of affection are considered taboo.

10. Systems that tolerate abuse are not interested in collecting their own history. They have things they would rather forget, and may try to erase their history. The famous novel about historical revisionism is *Nineteen Eighty-Four*, by George Orwell. Protagonist Winston Smith is an editor for the Ministry of Truth, and his job is to clip out

inconvenient facts and throw them down the memory hole. One of the steps to bring an abusive system to justice is to reconstruct its history.

To end on a positive note, here's the short list on the traits of healthy systems:

1. Individuality is respected; 2. Differences are tolerated; 3. Boundaries and roles are clearly defined; 4. Problem solving is open and valued; 5. Communication is responsive and accepting; 6. Qualified leadership; and 7. Healthy sense of humor, play, and fun, along with good work.

Appendix II
Child Abuse Defined

Child abuse (and neglect) is the parents' or guardians' failure to provide for a child's needs. The basic necessities of life include: appropriate clothing, including appropriate winter clothing and shoes; healthy food, playtime, time with parents; and decent living conditions, including personal hygiene supplies and a proper bed. Other needs include emotional support, spiritual and educational nurturing, and protection from physical and sexual harm.

Emotional Abuse

Abuse in this category includes humiliating or frightening punishments, verbal abuse, exposing children to violence such as spousal abuse in the household, witnessing abuse of other children, allowing children to use drugs or alcohol, and refusing to care for a child's special needs.

Physical Abuse

This includes inflicting physical pain by beating, hitting with an object, or any physical punishment besides a light spank on the bottom. Abuse may cause long-term spinal or nerve damage, or leave bruises and scars. Physical abuse does not necessarily leave marks.

Even if there is no lasting injury or scar, inflicting pain on others to extract compliance is immoral and cruel. Even ordinary spanking can prevent parent-child bonding and may teach children to solve their problems with physical violence.

Physical neglect includes refusal of, or delay in seeking medical care, abandonment, expulsion from home, not allowing a runaway to return home, and inadequate supervision.

Sexual Abuse

This category includes sexual touching, fondling, rape or attempted rape; exposing children to adult sexual materials or activity; peering into bathrooms or bedrooms to spy on children; having children pose, undress, or perform in a sexual fashion; taking provocative photos of children; pressuring children for sex; exhibitionism around children; or creating an atmosphere of sexual intimidation or humiliation.

Spiritual Abuse

Spiritual abuse includes using religious practices as punishments, forcing children to participate in rituals against their will, or scaring children with religious images. It may also include any form of abuse that endangers a child's well being, breaks a child's ability to trust, or makes a child feel unloved.

Educational Neglect

Educational neglect includes allowing chronic truancy, failure to enroll a child of school age, ignoring special educational needs, and enrolling children in dysfunctional schools that are not licensed and do not provide a suitable education for the child.

Appendix III
International Standards for Child Protection

Following is a collection of national and international documents that outline the standards for child protection, beginning in the 1920s.

The Declaration of the Rights of the Child

www.un.org/cyberschoolbus/humanrights/resources/plainchild.asp

Drafted by Eglantyne Jebb and adopted by the International Save the Children Union, Geneva, February 23, 1923, and endorsed by the League of Nations General Assembly on November 26, 1924. Proclaimed by UN General Assembly resolution 1386(XIV) of 20 November 1959. Adopted and opened for signature, ratification, and accession by UN General Assembly resolution 44/25 of November 20, 1998.

The Children's Bill of Rights April 20, 1996

www.newciv.org/ncn/cbor.html

Proclaimed on the Internet by the children of seven countries on three continents.

Communication Tips for Parents

American Psychological Association

www.apa.org/helpcenter/communication-parents.aspx

Ten Reasons Not to Hit Your Kids

by Jan Hunt, M.Sc., Director of The Natural Child Project

naturalchild.org/jan_hunt/tenreasons.html

Appendix IV
Resources

International Cultic Studies Association

icsahome.com

The ICSA is a network of people who study cultic groups. As the leading professional organization in the field, ICSA strives to understand questionable groups and to help the people who are harmed. ICSA holds conferences and workshops for former cult members and their families.

Surrealist.org

surrealist.org/links/cults.html

surrealist.org/gurukula/childabuseinfo.html

Find further writings by Nori Muster, as well as links, books, and resources for ex-cult members.

Safe Passage Foundation (SPF)

safepassagefoundation.org

Safe Passage Foundation provides resources for people raised in high-demand communities, including workshops for former members.

Bibliography

Forward, Susan and Buck, Craig. *Betrayal of Innocence: Incest and Its Devastation.* New York: Penguin Books, Ltd., 1988.

Jones, Celeste; Jones, Kristina, and Buhring, Juliana. *Not Without My Sister: The True Story of Three Girls Violated and Betrayed.* London: Harper Collins Element, 2007.

Kent, Stephen A., Ph.D. "Generational Revolt by the Adult Children of First-Generation Members of the Children of God/The Family." *Cultic Studies Review,* Vol. 3, No. 1, 2004:56-72.

Lalich, Janja and Tobias, Madeleine. *Take Back Your Life: Recovering from Cults and Abusive Relationships.* Berkeley: Bay Tree Publishing, 2006.

Miller, Alice. *The Untouched Key: Tracing Childhood Trauma in Creativity and Destructiveness*. New York: Doubleday, 1990.

Miller, Alice. *Breaking Down the Wall of Silence: The Liberating Experience of Facing Painful Truth*. New York: Meridian, 1993.

Muster, Nori. *Betrayal of the Spirit: My Life behind the Headlines of the Hare Krishna Movement*. Urbana and Chicago: University of Illinois Press, 1997.

Rhyne, Janie. *The Gestalt Art Experience: Creative Process and Expressive Therapy*. Chicago: Magnolia Street Publishers, 1984.

Rodriguez, Ricky. Suicide video transcript, 2005. Author's collection. Online, see: xfamily.org/index.php/Ricky_Rodriguez_Video_Transcript

Stevens, Barry. *Don't Push the River (it flows by itself)*. Lafayette, California: Real People Press, 1970.

Storr, Anthony. *Feet of Clay: Saints, Sinners, and Madmen: A Study of Gurus*. New York: Free Press Paperbacks published by Simon & Schuster, 1996.

Williams, Miriam. *Heaven's Harlots: My Fifteen Years as a Sacred Prostitute in the Children of God*. New York: William Morrow and

Company, Inc., 1998.

Life stories, written by the five participants in this collection: Flore A., Ph.D., Gina C., M.S., N.P., CNM, Ananda, Ann S., M.A., M.Phil., and Jane Doe (author's collection).

Endnotes

Author's Acknowledgements

1. Virginia M. Axline (1911-1988) is the author of *Play Therapy*, the seminal work on using Humanist, person-centered therapy with children.

2. The lecture by Dr. Adolf Ogi, where he expressed his vision for world peace, was at Badrutt's Palace in St. Moritz, Switzerland, October 2004.

Flore's Story

3. All quotations from the subjects are drawn from their autobiographical essays, unless otherwise noted.

4. The essay by Flore A. first appeared in the *Cultic Studies Review*, Vol. 2, No. 1, 2003.

5. Rev. Moon's mass weddings are well documented in the mainstream news, as well as cultic information sites such as

icsahome.com, freedomofmind.com, and culteducation.com. The most recent wedding, at this writing was March 3, 2015, when the UC wedded 3,800 couples in Gapyeong, South Korea. This was a just small number of couples compared to UC weddings of past decades.

6. Flore grew up with the label "unblessed child," because her parents' marriage was not blessed by Rev. Moon. Now the Unification Church calls such children Jacob's children, and there is less segregation than in the 1970s when Flore grew up.

7. For documentation on Moon's political and CIA connections, see: www.consortiumnews.com/archive/moon.html www.counterpunch.org/madsen01142003.html [counterpunch.org now offline], www.culteducation.com (Rick Ross site) www.freedomofmind.com (Steve Hassan site).

The Unification Church Website includes this statement by Moon: "Recently, the Republican party had an agenda to somehow pull America out of the United Nations. But I used the *Washington Times* to stop that evil attempt. I mobilized many ambassadors from around the world to exert their influence to stop it. UN ambassadors and American ambassadors met to discuss how to solve the United Nations' problems. The *Washington Times* pointed the direction for the future." See: www.tparents.org/moon-talks/sunmyungmoon97/SM970501.htm

Moon also referred to America as "Satan's Harvest" in the same article.

Robert Parry (Associated Press, *Newsweek*) outlines Rev. Moon's underworld and CIA ties in a special report about the *Washington Times*, published May 1, 2010, in *Consortium News*, see: www.consortiumnews.com/2010/050110.html

Exit counselor and former UC member, Steve Hassan, confirmed Rev. Moon's underworld ties in a June 2004 interview.

8. News of Rev. Moon's retirement appeared in *Time* magazine, in association with CNN and Associated Press, October 13, 2009. *Washington Times'* financial trouble was reported in the *Washington Post*, May 1, 2010, in an article by Ian Shapira. News of Moon buying the *Washington Times* back for $1 was reported in the Washington Post, November 3, 2010, in article by Ian Shapira.

Gina's Story

9. Some sources cite 1914 as the Maharishi Mahesh Yogi's birth date. However, Gina vetted *The New York Times* obituary, published Feb. 6, 2008, written by Lily Koppel, citing 1917 as the birth date.

10. Maharishi Vedic Education Development Corporation (MVED) governs the TM empire, markets the TM method through meditation-based universities, and manages the Ayur Vedic medicinal businesses, health spas, and other programs. They claim to have taught their methods to six million people.

11. The information about Maharishi and the Beatles is documented at songfacts.com, see: www.songfacts.com/detail.php?id=168

12. Joe Kellett, a former TM teacher and critic of the Maharishi and his methods, publishes his views at his Website, suggestibility.org

13. For more information, see "Lifton's Criteria of Thought Reform

As Applied to Transcendental Meditation, TM," by Gina Catena, M.S., posted at tmfree.blogspot.com/2007/01/liftons-thought-reform-criteria-applied.html Dr. Lifton's theories are outlined in his book, *Thought Reform and the Psychology of Totalism*, University of N. Carolina Press; reprint edition, 1989; original edition, W.W. Norton and Co. Inc., 1963.

14. Gina's reflections on her father's passing are from an email dated November 5, 2009; author's collection.

Ananda's Story

15. Ananda and other ISKCON children, and Nori Muster were interviewed and quoted in "Tortured Souls: Horribly abused children of the Hare Krishna movement seek justice—and peace—through a multimillion-dollar lawsuit," by Mark Donald, Dallas Observer, Thursday, December 6, 2001. www.dallasobserver.com/2001-12-06/news/tortured-souls/

16. ISKCON claimed millions of members around the world, but they are counting people as members who may have simply seen the mantra performed live, given a donation, or attended the temple on a part time basis. Actual core membership of fulltime followers has dwindled since the peak in the mid-1970s.

17. The ISKCON zonal gurus who left within the first ten years for corruption were: Hamsadutta, Kirtanananda, Bhavananda, Ramesvara, and Jayatirtha. Since then, two more left, Harikesha and Bhagavan, both for personal reasons. In 2002, Tamal Krishna died while still a guru in good standing. There are currently three of the

original eleven remaining as gurus: Hridayananda, Jayapataka, and Satsvarupa.

Nori Muster's essays on ISKCON are indexed at icsahome.com and norimuster.com. Her papers and writer's journals are held in the American Religions Collection at the University of California, Santa Barbara (UCSB). *Betrayal of the Spirit* is now available as an e-book, as well as paperback.

18. The *Children of ISKCON vs. ISKCON* lawsuit cites 1990 as the end of systemic child abuse in ISKCON, as does a zero tolerance for child abuse petition posted at the ISKCON-related Website, Chakra.org. However, systemic abuse started to end in 1986, so some people cite 1986 as the end of ISKCON's systemic abuse of children.

19. For further information about ISKCON's under-aged brides, see *Betrayal of the Spirit*, chapter eight, "Who's Watching the Children?"

20. In an interview, the children of Krishna explained the punishment for outsiders who molest ISKCON children; author's collection.

21. The guru Ramesvara publicly denied any connection to the Laguna Beach drug ring or the gangland murder associated with that operation. See "Kulik Tied Close to Krishna Boss" (referring to Ramesvara in the article), *Orange County Register*, Nov. 10, 1977, by Larry Welborn.

22. The GBC resolutions against child abuse appear in the 1990 minutes, see resolution 119:

pratyatosa.com/GBCRES/GBCRES1990.htm

23. "Children of the Ashram," by Rathunath Anudas, *ISKCON Youth Veterans* newsletter, Vol. IV, Aug. 1990, supplement, pp. 28-49. An indexed and lightly edited version is available online, see: surrealist.org/gurukula/timeline/children.html

24. Ten former *gurukula* students gave three hours of testimony before the North American GBC meeting held May 17-18, 1996, in Alachua, Florida. At that meeting, the GBC members said they acknowledged the extent of the abuse and formed Children of Krishna, Inc. An editorial in the Spring/Summer 1996 issue of *Priti-laksanam* about the GBC meeting, said:

"*Sannyasis* [elder GBC members] cried. You could see the shame in some of the men's eyes. I believe it was even more than the awful threat of lawsuits that spurred these men, so committed to ISKCON, to go beyond passing resolutions." In 1998, the GBC formed the ISKCON Child Protection Office, headed by Doctor of Social Work David Wolf (then Dhira Govinda Dasa, in the organization).

25. The V.O.I.C.E. Website is now offline, but excerpts are posted here: surrealist.org/gurukula/timeline/docs.html#23

26. "Child Abuse in the Hare Krishna Movement: 1971-1986," by Burke Rochford, Ph.D., appeared in the *ISKCON Communications Journal*, Vol. 6, No. 1, June 1998, pp. 43-70.

27. The headline "Hare Krishnas lift the lid on history of child abuse." appeared over a Religious News Service report by Ira Rifkinc, 1998.

28. Details of the *Children of ISKCON vs. ISKCON* case settlement

are from "L.A. abuse deal is deep, not fatal blow," Associated Press, June 17, 2007.

29. For a full timeline of *gurukula* abuse and the *Children of ISKCON vs. ISKCON* lawsuit, see: surrealist.org/gurukula/timeline/ and surrealist.org/gurukula/timeline/lawsuit.html" target="_blank">http://surrealist.org/gurukula/timeline/lawsuit.html

30. Michael Gressett's dissertation is, *From Krishna cult to American church: The dialectical quest for spiritual dwelling in the modern Krishna movement in the west,* University of Florida, 2009. See: gradworks.umi.com/33/85/3385932.html

For a discussion of possible continued abuse, see: *BVPS at Mayapur Gurkula?* a forum for former *gurukula* students. Chakra Discussions, chakra.org, thread started October 19, 2003. Also see *Alleged Abuse And Cover-Up In Vrindavan Gurukul,* by Bhima-karma Das (New Vrindavan Gurukul Alumni), *Vaishnava News Network* (VNN), Sept. 28, 2004, http://www.vnn.org/world/WD0409/WD28-8710.html [this Website is now offline] See also, Chakra.org "Zero Tolerance for Child Abuse in ISKCON" petition, with the following provision: "Whereas there is still at least one person in the position of Guru and *Sannyasi* who has played a major role in the history of child abuse in ISKCON and who to date has been supported by a section of the Governing body of ISKCON." It said "at least one," but reports at VNN.org and Chakra.org say that more than one pedophile has tried to come back and there may be more still active within the hierarchy.

Ann's Story

31. The official AR Websites state these as Siegel's principles (see aestheticrealism.org and aestheticrealism.net).

32. This statement critical of the organization, but not the philosophy, was made by Michael Bluejay, a former member of Aesthetic Realism, see: michaelbluejay.com/x/ For more critical reviews of AR, see *A former Aesthetic Realism student involved for over a decade speaks out*, written January 24, 2005, michaelbluejay.com/x/statements/ar-exposed.html. This and the other anonymous quotes about AR come from this essay.

33. All quoted statements from Ann S., come from a paper she wrote for a meeting of the Cult Information Services, Inc. (CIS), in New Jersey in 2002; also in statements she wrote for this book in an email dated January 17, 2011, and in telephone interviews with Nori Muster in January 2011.

34. See icsahome.com for information about their second generation workshops.

35. For more about the abuse cycle in cults, see: Ward, David. (2000). "Domestic violence as a cultic system," *Cultic Studies Journal*, 17, 42-45. Ramirez Boulette, Teresa, & Andersen, Susan (1986). "Mind control and the battering of women," *Cultic Studies Journal*, 3(2), 25-35.

Jane's Story

36. In 2007, journalist Don Lattin published his book-length exposé about the Children of God, *Jesus Freaks: A True Story of Murder*

and Madness on the Evangelical Edge (HarperOne).

37. Ex-cult.org confirms, "In Letter number 302C, written March 21, 1974, Berg proclaimed that God had now seen fit to trust the COG/Family with new freedoms which Christians of past ages had not been mature enough to handle. He was, of course, referring to free sex." See: culthelp.info (search keyword "302C").

38. *Liberty or Stumbling Block?*, issued in November 1986, is available at this ex-member Website:
www.xfamily.org/index.php/Liberty_or_Stumbling_Block

39. *Heavens Harlots*, by Miriam Williams (1998).

40. Ibid., p. 8.

41. For information on Children of God child pornography, see: Kent, 2004. Dr. Kent, Department of Sociology, University of Alberta, Edmonton, has documented pornography in the Children of God.
www.xfamily.org/index.php/Generational_Revolt_by_the_Adult_Ch
ildren_of_First-
Generation_Members_of_the_Children_of_God/The_Family The University holds examples of Children of God pornography, because it is illegal for an individual to possess these materials. If there were a lawsuit against the organization, the plaintiffs could subpoena these materials from the University.

42. The theory on the origin of David Berg's twisted theology is drawn from "Lustful Prophet: A Psychosexual Historical Study of the Children of God's Leader, David Berg," by Dr. Stephen A. Kent, published in the *Cultic Studies Journal*, Volume 11, No. 2 (1994).

See: www.arts.ualberta.ca/~skent/Linkedfiles/lustfulprophet.htm

43. Rodriguez suicide video transcript, p. 6.

44. Ibid., p. 12.

45. *Children of God: Lost and Found*, premiered on Cinemax Sept. 5, 2007.

46. Mary McNamara's review appeared in the *Los Angeles Times* on Sept. 5, 2007.

47. Ibid. *Los Angeles Times*, Sept. 5, 2007.

48. This quote is drawn from an anonymous Internet posting dated April 26, 2005, which can be found as a comment here: www.movingon.org/article.asp?sID=3&Cat=39&ID=2937 [post is off line].

49. *Not Without My Sister* is an autobiographical account written by three sisters who grew up in the Children of God.

50. Jones, Jones & Buhring, p. 203.

51. This quote is drawn from an anonymous Internet posting dated April 26, 2005, from movingon.org [post is off line]. 52. Lalich, p. 264.

53. Information on whether to confront an abuser is drawn from "Male Survivors of Incest and Sexual Child Abuse," by John W. Wilson, see: www.theviproom.com/visions/sexabuse.htm

Conclusion

54. Anna Freud, daughter of Sigmund Freud, was the first to name what she called "identification with the aggressor" in her 1936 book, *The Ego and the Mechanisms of Defense*. New York: International

Universities Press.

55. Robert Lifton's *Eight Criteria for Thought Reform* are: 1. Milieu Control; 2. Mystical Manipulation (Planned Spontaneity); 3. The Demand for Purity; 4. Confession; 5. Sacred Science; 6. Loading the Language; 7. Doctrine Over Person; and 8. Dispensing of Existence. For a full explanation of Lifton's criteria, see Dr. Robert J. Lifton's *Criteria for Thought Reform*, a study guide available at icsahome.com/

56. The American Psychiatric Association publishes the *Diagnostic and Statistical Manual (DSM)*, the handbook of psychological diagnoses for insurance purposes.

57. The term "trust bandits" is attributed to Magrid and McKelvey, as cited on p. 61 and in footnote 22, chapter 4, p. 348, of *Take Back Your Life*, by Janja Lalich.

58. The term "confidence tricksters" is used to describe dangerous charismatic figures, as cited in Storr, p. 153.

59. Alice Miller, 1990, p. 162.

60. The organization that advocates separation of adults and children is www.darkness2light.org/

61. There have been no definitive studies, but the figures stated are based on answers from two prominent researchers in this field: Lois Kendall, Ph.D., and Livia Bardin, M.S.W. Dr. Kendall found in a study of one group that seventy-four percent of children left the sect at or below the age of nineteen. Two further studies by Dr. Kendall examining second generation former members of a variety of groups and recorded the average age of leaving for the second generation as

being twenty-one and twenty-four years of age. Bardin estimated that one and a half million children are currently growing up in cults worldwide. If distributed equally by age, approximately 57,750 would reach age eighteen each year. See: "Recognizing and working with an underserved culture; Child protection and cults," *Journal of Public Child Welfare*, 3.2 (April-June 2009), L. Bardin, pp. 114-138.

62. The Janie Rhyne quotation comes from her book, *The Gestalt Art Experience* (1984), page 47.

63. The Barry Stevens quotation comes from her book, *Don't Push the River* (1970), page 107.

64. The *Washington Post* published an article on the University of Arizona's expulsion of the Faith Christian Ministry after dangerous cult behavior came to light. See, " 'Love-bombing' group at University of Arizona called cult, thrown out of religious council," by Susan Svrluga, *Washington Post*, April 1, 2015.

About the Author

Nori Muster has been a journalist and writer since 1981 and holds a master's degree from Western Oregon University. Her first book, *Betrayal of the Spirit: My Life behind the Headlines of the Hare Krishna Movement* (University of Illinois Press, 1997), documents ten years in ISKCON. Her master's thesis on using art therapy with juveniles is posted at her Website, norimuster.com.

About the Cover

The image on the cover is the Rider Waite tarot card, Justice, which dates back to 1909. The High Priestess is seated between two pillars, holding the scales of karma in one hand and the sword of judgment in the other. Justice is the universal moral principle that gives every person the results of his or her works. Bad behavior invites undesirable results; innocence is restored and protected. Author's note: "The first time I saw this image associated with the children of cults was in 2002, when a woman who grew up in ISKCON used it for her cult survivors' web ring. Later, when she gave up her responsibilities as the web ring coordinator, I asked her blessings to continue to use the image to symbolize recovery from child abuse.

Made in the USA
San Bernardino, CA
11 November 2017